P9-CEN-515

Crime in
Urban Society

Joseph S. Clark
David Fellman
Kenneth McLennan
W. Walter Menninger
Albert J. Reiss, Jr.
Simon Rottenberg
Arthur J. Sills

Barbara N. McLennan
Editor

Foreword by
Ramsey Clark

Crime in Urban Society

The Dunellen Company, Inc., New York

International Standard Book Number 0-8424-0004-4.

Library of Congress catalog card number 73-122595.

Printed in the United States of America.

Designed by Anspach Grossman Portugal, Inc.

Contents

List of Tables and Figures

Foreword

Of the many causes of crime in America, urbanization is among the least understood and most significant. Our crime is overwhelmingly an urban phenomena. We must know why and what can be done to prevent it. In cities with more than 250,000 people, robberies occur ten times more often proportionately than in their surrounding suburbs and are thirty-five times more common per capita than in outlying rural areas. The risk of being murdered is four to five times greater for the urban dweller than for his suburban neighbor. Auto thefts are fourteen times more frequent per capita in cities than in the country.

Statistics which compare only urban and rural crime are facts that are the enemy of truth. Only when we recognize the great concentration of crime in certain parts of our cities can we glean its true meaning. Within every major urban area of America there are thousands crammed together, living in poverty. There infant mortality is four times the cities' average, life expectancy seven years less, and mental retardation eight times more common. Per capita income averages 60 percent of that for the whole city; unemployment is four times greater; and the jobs held are menial —domestic servant, janitor, car washer. Formal educational attainment in the slums is four years less, on the average, than for all the citizens of the same city, but in quality and classroom turbulence the difference is vast. The houses and tenements are the oldest, most crowded in the city and dangerous to health and life. Fire alarms are ten times more frequent, and the people who live there—perhaps 10 or 20 percent of the city's population—experience two thirds of the arrests and suffer three fourths of the crime of the whole city.

The cost of police and their presence are several times higher per capita than for the newer parts of town. The people there live in an uneasy order, but largely without law. Their rights are generally unenforceable, and they are often harassed by the law itself. The police are usually alien in spirit and afraid of the people they must serve. Most crime is never reported.

The system of criminal justice will never contain more than a fraction of the crime that can occur among an urban people. Today, it is doubtful that police investigations, district attorneys' prosecutions and courts' adjudications achieve one conviction for every fifty serious crimes. A tenfold improvement in performance—impossible to achieve—would still be a long way from raising the odds of apprehension to a deterrent among even the rational who are capable of committing crime.

To substantially reduce crime, we must care for all of our people. Good health, sound education, meaningful employment, decent housing, guaranteed income, and an environment that is compatible with human dignity will be essential to a reverence for life. Without reverence for life, we will continue our violent ways.

These are the immense needs of our mass, technologically advanced, urban society. Until they are fulfilled, the pollutions of anxiety, frustration, and violence will grow with the increasing pressures of population, scientific discovery, and dehumanization.

Our capacity to meet these needs is clear. We fail to release half the energies of our people. By leasing those energies, we can provide the necessities of urban life, which far exceed those of simpler times; provide the chance for individual fulfillment for millions now conditioned to antisocial attitudes; and master the fact of our interdependence. In modern urban society, hundreds of thousands must perform effectively for any to find an acceptable quality of life.

In the meantime, we must overcome the blight of decades of neglect of the system of criminal justice. We must recognize that medical-social problems, such as alcoholism, drug addiction, and mental disturbance, cannot be solved by guns and clubs—and that they are the major contributors to urban crime. Police salaries must be increased and high standards for personnel rigorously maintained, so that professional skills can be brought to the prevention and control of crime—with strict adherence to the rule of law. Science and technology must be directed to solving the problems of criminal conduct and improving the performance of the system of criminal justice. Courts and prosecutors must be provided with the resources and skills necessary to assure Constitutional guarantees of fair and speedy trials. Billions must be spent on rehabilitation of repeat offenders, whose crimes account for 80 percent of all serious offenses. Jails and prisons—which manufacture crime—must be leveled and new community facilities developed that can protect the public by the only way that works—the rehabilitation of offenders. We must move into high-crime areas of our major cities and work with all our might to give children presently condemned to lives of crime their chance—before they fall into patterns of delinquency. Health services, intense

Head Start efforts, child-care facilities for children from broken families, special tutoring, reinforced teaching in preschool and grammar school years, programs that prevent dropouts, who account for 90 percent of the juvenile offenses—these are but a few of the things we must do.

Crime is the ultimate human degradation. It reflects the character of a people. We have no higher obligation than to reduce its presence to the lowest possible levels. We know how. The questions is whether we care.

Ramsey Clark

Washington, D.C.
June, 1970

Acknowledgments

This book was made possible by the generous support of the Department of Political Science, Center for the Study of Federalism, and the College of Liberal Arts, Temple University. The editor would like to extend grateful thanks to all persons who contributed to the presentations and discussions upon which this volume is based.

In particular, the editor wishes to acknowledge the active participation and financial support of Harry A. Bailey, Jr., Chairman of the Department of Political Science, Temple University, and of Daniel J. Elazar, Director, and Joseph Zikmund II, Acting Director, Center for the Study of Federalism, Temple University. The editor also would like to acknowledge the very generous financial support made available by George W. Johnson, Dean, and George Harrington, Associate Dean, College of Liberal Arts, Temple University.

The comments of many distinguished persons were helpful in the final formulation of this volume. The editor would like to thank especially the following persons, whose ideas were incorporated into the last chapter: Monroe Berkowitz, Department of Economics, Rutgers—the State University; J. R. Norsworthy and Paul Seidenstat, Department of Economics, Temple University; Henry J. Abraham, Department of Political Science, University of Pennsylvania; and J. Shane Creamer, Director, Pennsylvania Crime Commission. The editor would also like to thank Robert Haakenson, of Smith, Kline and French Corp., for making available the original data on the demographic characteristics of the ghetto.

The editor wishes to extend grateful appreciation to John F. Adams, Assistant Vice President for Finance and Assistant Treasurer, Temple University; George F. Rohrlich, Department of Economics, Temple University; and Seymour L. Wolfbein, Dean, School of Business Administration, Temple University, whose help and advice made the publication of this book possible. The help of the secretarial staff at the Department of Political Science, Temple University, particularly that of Doris Shinn, Linda Scherr, and Linda Herko, was essential in processing the original manuscript. Joan Trafton Ricci of The Dunellen Company deserves special mention for her help and efficiency in bringing the book to final publication.

Introduction

Americans are today very concerned about the apparent spread of crime and growing brutality of life in American cities. Such slogans as "Law and Order," "Safety in the Streets," and "Support the Police" have been central debating points in many recent elections and were widely heard in the presidential election campaign of 1968. Americans appear to be convinced that crime is spreading at a rapid pace and that prevailing political authorities are either unable or unwilling to cope with the problem.

Though many citizens share a common concern about and interest in the supposed spread of crime, there still remains a broad area of misunderstanding and vagueness about the concept in the popular mind. Under the rubric of "crime" such disparate acts as racial disorders, student violence, anti-war protests, marches, demonstrations, and riots have colored many of the legal protest activities of certain groups with the stigma of criminality. Any challenge to local authorities or traditional concepts of lawful practice is widely held to be unlawful and somehow "criminal" by many citizens in the United States today.

Of course, there exists a broad literature on the subject of crime, and crime is constantly being investigated by many government agencies. Scholars in the field distinguish crime into many distinct categories and refer to these categories in the way that medical scholars will treat different diseases—each crime has its own symptoms, causes, effects, and, presumably, cures. "Crime," as a broad catch-all phrase, is about as useful to criminologists as the term "disease" is to doctors.

Crime has consequently been subdivided into such categories as violent personal crime, occasional property crime, occupational crime, political crime, public order crime, conventional crime, organized crime, and professional crime.[1] Another categorization, employed by the President's Commission on Law Enforcement and Administration of Justice, divides crime under the chapter headings "Juvenile Delinquency," "Organized Crime," "Narcotics and Drug Abuse," and "Drunkenness Offenses."[2]

The commission noted in its report that there were more than 2,800 federal crimes and many more state and local ones. The most serious crimes, about which citizens were personally most concerned, were those listed by the FBI's Uniform Crime Reports (UCR) as "crimes of violence against the person" and "property crime." These in turn are normally broken down by the UCR into such categories as willful homicide, forcible rape, aggravated assault, robbery, burglary, larceny of $50 and over, and motor vehicle theft.[3] The only uniform characteristic of all these crimes is that each involves the violation of some written law. A criminal, no matter what his crime may be, is someone who is convicted of violating a law, i.e., the written word of some legislative or judicial body.

Approaches to the Problem of Crime

Every crime involves a number of direct and indirect participants. Every crime has a perpetrator and a victim; every crime, because defined by the law, also involves the moral authority of the entire society. Society or "the people" are the moral basis for the legal code and the source of legitimacy for the entire political system. Any crime, because it challenges the law, thus challenges the greater society.

The legal system and law enforcement authorities are employed by society through the use of tax revenues. Crime is costly to society not only because it attacks persons and property, but also because society pays for the whole array of law enforcement and crime prevention activities undertaken by government. The more government does about crime, the more society must pay for these activities. Thus, any discussion of the costs of crime must assess not only the cost to the victim but all the costs, direct and indirect, in the procedures of American criminal justice.

The costs of crime are also individual. The criminal or potential criminal is himself paying the psychological costs of maladjustment to his environment. He is reacting to a variety of personal background factors which have shaped his behavior and personality. No complete picture of crime can ignore the fact that criminal behavior is exhibited by individuals who are caught up in special kinds of personal difficulties and in situations which are very complex and far from easy to investigate. These behavioral causes of crime are difficult for society, at the present stage of science and technology, to remedy. Indeed, it is hard enough today to bring the recognition of environmental and psychological factors into any public dialogue on the crime problem.

Thus, there are many gaps and much misinformation in the present discussion of crime in the United States. Law enforcement practices are frequently outmoded and new legislation in this area is difficult to achieve.

We have an ancient penal system, rigid and inflexible police departments, an archaic court system—but very modern, up-to-date criminals. Much of what is publicly spoken is directed at today's problems, but much of what is done follows procedures laid down many years ago.

Understanding the Crime Problem

The present volume presents a series of critical essays on the subject of crime by eminent specialists and practitioners in the field. These essays are unified in their purpose, in the sense that they all challenge the prevailing misunderstandings in the crime debate and attempt to demonstrate where there are substantial gaps in our understanding and treatment of the problem.

In Part 1, "The Nature and Extent of Crime," Dr. Walter Menninger of the Menninger Foundation introduces the discussion with an inquiry into the psychodynamic roots of urban crime. Dr. Menninger challenges many simplistic assumptions current today and attempts to demonstrate the great complexity of the problem by focusing on its psychological sources. Dr. Albert J. Reiss, Jr., of the University of Michigan, follows with a fundamental challenge to the entire system of reporting and assessing crime statistics in the United States. Dr. Reiss questions not only the statistical presumptions implicit in today's crime reports but also challenges the interpretations of these statistics. Many basic attitudes with respect to the cost of crime are further challenged by Dr. Simon Rottenberg of Duke University. Dr. Rottenberg looks at the problem from a completely economic viewpoint, discussing the actual distribution of the effects of crime as well as the real economic choices available to society in this area.

Part 2, "Current Practice with Respect to Crime," contains three essays which indicate the gaps as well as the accomplishments in current governmental practice with respect to crime. Attorney General Arthur J. Sills of New Jersey begins with a discussion of the problems of state governments in fighting organized crime. Attorney General Sills indicates the extent to which states may legally go in combating crime and also makes a series of recommendations as to what may be done to improve the capacity of the states in this vital area. Senator Joseph S. Clark follows with a discussion of the role of federal government in combating violence in the United States. Senator Clark is as much concerned with the areas in which the federal authorities have not acted as with the areas in which they have. He is highly critical of many federal practices and proposals, particularly with respect to gun control. The discussion of current governmental action is completed by Dr. David Fellman of the University of Wisconsin in "The Supreme Court's Changing Views of the Criminal Defendant's Rights." Dr. Fellman evaluates the long-term trends in American criminal law and specifically assesses the major ground-breaking decisions of the Warren Court. The theory upon which American legal practice with respect to crime is based is clearly described and evaluated by Dr. Fellman.

The final chapter of this volume, "Public Policy and the Control of Crime," summarizes the major proposals and recommendations made by the foregoing specialists. The chapter also presents some current information on specific areas of crime and draws further policy implications from these data.

Notes

1. Marshall B. Clinard and Richard Quimey, *Criminal Behavior Systems* (New York: Holt, Rinehart and Winston, Inc., 1967).
2. President's Commission on Law Enforcement and the Administration of Justice, *The Challenge of Crime in a Free Society* (Washington, D.C.: U.S. Government Printing Office, 1967).
3. Ibid, p. 18.

Part 1: The Nature and Extent of Crime

1

The Roots of Urban Crime: A Psychodynamic Perspective

W. Walter Menninger, M.D.

It is the challenge of understanding that piques the interest of the psychiatrist. A psychodynamic perspective which provides an analytic perspective on human functioning can help us to understand some of the irrationality of human nature.

Until the advent of psychoanalysis, the approach to psychiatric understanding was limited to a descriptive level. The chief interest in mental disorders was in outlining symptoms and making word pictures of the various clinical syndromes. As a result of such an approach, various emotional disorders were described and redescribed, with a great deal of detail as to the minute variations of each symptom. It was Freud who prompted a shift in emphasis by attempting to understand the meaning and motivation of symptoms and behavior. In contrast to being descriptive, the approach became dynamic. There were attempts to answer such questions as Why does the person develop this symptom? What does it mean? What part does it play in the total life picture of the individual? About what kind of conflict does this behavior center?

The analogy has been made of comparing the descriptive method to looking at broken-down automobiles in a junkyard and carefully classifying them by the nature of the "wreck." The dynamic approach instead studies the machine in motion and assesses how the parts are interrelated and what actually happened to cause the wreck. Obviously, if we are to decrease the frequency of wrecks, we must examine the process which leads to a wreck.

The psychodynamic perspective has some other givens. An important aspect of this perspective is the manner of viewing crime and criminal behavior. In the common parlance and common understanding, crime is simply defined as breaking the law, but there are, in fact, many different kinds of crime—simple, complex, minor, major. Generally our attention is drawn to the violent crimes. These are the crimes that evoke the emotions and stir up our anxiety. The attention they receive is much like the attention given the cancers and other serious diseases in medicine. We usually think that such crime does not affect us but is the concern of others.

Much time and energy are spent detailing the statistics of crimes—with the epitome being the FBI's "crime clock" in Washington, ticking off its murder, robbery, etc., every so many minutes. The emphasis again is on events that presumably happen to others, and the immediate relevance to all of us is not very clear, aside from making us more fearful of our fellow man. The statistical efforts call to mind the same kind of statistics that are developed about the incidence of mental illness, which is another human condition that we generally think happens only to others. All of us, however, at some time or other, have emotional upsets, depressions, blue funks, temper tantrums, or some equivalent emotional disorder—in the same way that we all have colds, upset stomachs, headaches, and other minor illnesses. Relatively few of us develop serious diseases, and when we do, they are generally transient. We usually don't stay physically ill, nor do we stay emotionally ill.

To reiterate the perspective I wish to take, let me quote some of Dr. Karl Menninger's opening remarks in **The Human Mind:**

> When a trout rising to a fly gets hooked on a line and finds himself unable to swim about freely, he begins a fight which results in struggles and splashes and sometimes an escape. Often, of course, the situation is too tough for him.
>
> In the same way the human being struggles with his environment and with the hooks that catch him. Sometimes he masters his difficulties; sometimes they are too much for him. His struggles are all that the world sees and it usually misunderstands them. It is hard for a free fish to understand what is happening to a hooked one.
>
> Sooner or later, however, most of us get hooked. How much of a fight we have on our hands then depends upon the hook, and, of course, on us. If the struggle gets too violent, if it throws us out of the water, if we run afoul of other strugglers, we become "cases" in need of help and understanding.[1]

As with mental and emotional disorders, all of us have also been criminals. We have all violated the law—and probably we still do. The greatest differentiation is not in the breaking of the law but in the judgment of when we can break the law and get away with it. It is knowing when we can speed without being caught, or which deductions will get by, or what income we can hide. In the process of growing up, most of us, somewhere along the line, have tested the legal authorities, and we may have committed a moderately serious offense as well as many petty offenses. Throughout all this, we may or may not have been caught, and even if caught, we may not have been called to task very severely.

It is in the context of the universality of criminal behavior—if only on a most minor level—that we wish to address the subject of crime and then consider some particular aspects of urban life that affect crime.

Since we are not yet in "1984," crime involves action. We have come close to "thought crime," but essentially we are speaking of behavior of individuals. The challenge is to understand that all actions of any individual can be related in some meaningful way to that individual as a whole.

The Personality-Environment Struggle

As suggested by the "hooked fish" analogy of Dr. Karl Menninger, every human being is faced with a constant struggle to survive. This struggle may be characterized as the personality–environment struggle. That is, from the instant we are conceived to the day we die, we are involved in a constant process of adjusting and adapting to the situation in which we live. This is an interactional process between our total organism and the environment. The term "personality," in this context, refers to the organism—all that we are, have been, hope to be; our hopes, fears, physical state, memories, knowledge; in short, what we think of when we think of ourselves.

This personality-environment struggle can be depicted somewhat diagrammatically as a constant collision between us and our environment. Our personality is constantly changing, but so is the environment. Within a short period of time, one may be listening to a tedious lecture, hearing some disturbing news about crime, enjoying a luncheon with friends, reading an intriguing book. Each situation is different, and the person conducts himself differently and reacts differently.

Within the steady interaction of the person and his environment there is a constant process of adjustment, with a thousand and one little struggles within the one big struggle for human survival. Many, perhaps most, of the facets of the struggle are dealt with in ways of which we are unaware. There are the conscious struggles: How are we going to get all the work done? When are we going to write that long overdue letter? How are we going to squeeze out some more money from the budget to buy that needed appliance? How are we going to clear up that misunderstanding in the family? Less apparent but more vital are the many unconscious struggles, which take place on many different levels. There are the physiological adjustments—the automatic adaptation of the body to keep the body temperature constant, or to keep the body chemistry within that very narrow range of acid-base balance which is compatible with life, or to redirect the circulation of the blood supply to the intestines after we eat or to our muscles after we exercise. There are also myriad automatic psychological adjustments, which in many cases are the result of our life experience. On one level, we can become aware of many noises and stimuli if we attend to them, but usually we automatically screen out all but the most important. When we drive a car, much of our behavior after years of driving becomes automatic, so that we can attend to other matters at the same time. On a deeper level, there are many inner conflicts with which we struggle that affect our adjustment but of which we are not consciously aware.

It is the sum of our coping with these struggles which we may consider as representing our adjustment, or vital balance.

Again, if one is to diagram this adjustment process, one must be aware that there are two possible outcomes to the personality-environment struggle: success, which we may term adjustment, and failure, which we may term maladjustment. We have all witnessed differences in the reactions of personalities to the onslaughts of the environment. Some people can take the loss of their homes and all belongings in stride. Others will go to pieces at an imaginary loss. Everyone, of course, does have his limit—not many personalities can still be in there adjusting after a full-speed, head-on collision with as solid a piece of environment as a 10-ton truck.

Our failures, our maladjustments, are manifested in behaviors or reactions which can be broadly characterized in one of two ways: a reaction of flight or a reaction of fight. If we meet a situation which is too tough for us to manage or accept, we may dodge it or run away from it, or we may try to attack it in any one of several ways. In the flight reaction, it is usually the personality which suffers, as in sickness, drunkenness, loss of standing, loss of prestige. How much the personality suffers is a function of the demands made by the environment and the strength of the personality. The range of flight reactions is wide—from sulking, depression, daydreaming, and taking a walk, to retreat into one's own world in severe mental illness or running away physically to escape the situation. In the fight reaction, it is usually the environment that suffers. Few, if any, of us have not reached the point of just lashing out at the environment to try and change it or destroy it, whether yelling at the kids to stop their infernal racket, or being frustrated beyond our level of tolerance. A considerable number of personalities attack the environment in an illegal way—and thus become criminals.

Thus, in viewing the personality-environment struggle, crime and criminal behavior can be placed in a broader context, the life-adjustment process. Like illness, crime may be considered a manifestation of maladjustment in this process. This is not to say all criminals are ill, although many are; but illness, both physical and emotional, is distinct from crime as a type of maladjustment. More important, criminal behavior is behavior which is an attempt at adaptation, albeit a socially undesirable and unacceptable attempt. It may well be the best attempt possible for the offender, a reflection of his inadequacy to adapt successfully to his world, at least as viewed by the larger society. However, he himself may not perceive the adjustment as unsuccessful. And one must be reminded that we all have violated the law in our adjustment attempts—whether it is speeding to make up for being late to an appointment, or pilfering some supplies for our own personal use, or the like.

Personality: Basic Tenets

In order to make sense of irrational behavior, one must acknowledge some basic tenets, some key principles which provide the basis for understanding the functioning of personality. Criminal behavior is an aberration, an extreme on a continuum of behavior which all of us manifest. Therefore, to talk about the roots of the aberration, we must examine the roots of all human personality functioning—thinking, as is done throughout this paper, of "personality" as a representation of the total person and his functioning.

The first principle necessary for understanding is acknowledgment of the importance of feelings, of emotions, in determining human behavior. Man is called a rational animal, and yet as we look about us, we must inevitably have doubts. It is more appropriate to call us emotional animals. Clearly, the most powerful forces that motivate us are our emotions, which are not especially rational. While we may explain to ourselves why we think we do what we do, quite often our explanations are rather transparent. It is impressive to observe the careful rationalizations which we make to justify our actions, our prejudices, our feelings. More often than not, the truth is that we don't know why we do some things. This is quite true of many criminal acts. The check forger who seeks to pass far more checks than he actually needs—indeed, who keeps passing them just to see how many he can get away with; the bank robber who isn't content with just robbing the bank but must murder some of the personnel in the bank; the shoplifter who has money in his pocket to pay for the goods but responds to the impulse to take the goods without paying— these are persons who are responding to some irrational, emotional need.

Our emotions thus represent powerful forces in our lives. They are the complicating factors in our adjustment process. These emotional drives have been variously postulated, but they may be conceptualized in terms of the two great emotional experiences, love and hate. Open expression of these emotions in their "raw" form—by sexual activity or destructive violence—is socially acceptable only in carefully circumscribed circumstances. Thus much of our growing up is a process of containing these forces, or learning to modify them so that they can be expressed in an acceptable manner, through work and play, in our relationships with others.

We have no trouble observing open emotional behavior in our children, when we look. Actually, we often see only what we want to see and wear blinders to screen out the disquieting or unacceptable things. You don't have to observe children very long to perceive their self-centered and destructive behavior. Give the average toy to a two-year-old and see how long it survives his pushing, pulling, smashing, and throwing. There is some justification in labeling this age group the "terrible twos." Notice the interplay between older children—grasping, hitting, shrieking. We may label this "roughhousing," but it generally ends with someone being hurt. One might say that the only reason we can tolerate the existence of children, aside from some other significant gratifications they give us, is that physically we can control them.

Because of the reactions we experience from open display of love or hate, we tend to keep these emotions under wraps. This process occurs as we grow up. As adults, we often delude ourselves by denying or overlooking the fact that we continue to be strongly affected by these same drives. We tend to hide from ourselves the fact that we are no less subject to the power of these basic emotional strivings as adults than we were as children. The difference is that we have developed ways to cope with those drives.

It must be noted that thoughts and feelings can be every bit as powerful in affecting human behavior as is behavior itself. In other words, very often what really happens in our life is not half so important as what we think and believe happens. We may get into a terrific argument with someone over a disputed event, and our reaction is a function of what we believe we saw or felt to be so, not what actually happened. In clinical work, this is a matter simply of recognizing the validity of psychological data. When a patient reports one thing and a relative reports the event differently, the psychiatrist must acknowledge that what the patient reports is what is "true" for the patient. While an offender may distort or falsify his view of events, generally he does so to justify to himself a rational basis for his behavior. How he perceives the world is an important factor in determining how he behaves.

A second tenet in understanding all human behavior is the recognition of some of the basic beginning points in personality development. We all start from a common beginning at birth. When the infant is born, we can be sure that he doesn't understand what is happening; his responses are instinctual. He has no capacity for rationally and logically assessing what is going on; his central nervous system is not yet mature, so he is unable to integrate his experiences systematically, much less perceive them in much order. The infant is a biological organism with only the most rudimentary of emotional and psychological equipment. His interest in life could be formulated rather simply: to gain satisfaction and to find relief from any discomfort which he perceives. One might postulate that the infant's only motive in life is to have the basic instincts satisfied.

In his early months, the infant gives nothing to anyone else; he makes no attempt to please anyone. One may say that the infant operates on the principle of gaining all the pleasure he can and, so far as possible, avoiding all displeasure and pain. This principle of operation we term the "pleasure principle." In operating on this basis, the infant, as he develops, is clearly self-centered and seeks immediate and direct satisfaction of whatever impulse strikes him. He has no real conception of nor concern for what may result from his action beyond the satisfaction of his impulse. Frustration of a wish is protested mightily. The child sees himself as the center of the universe, and everything revolves around him.

When the child is frustrated or hurt, the response is simplistic. When he suffers pain, he wants to let others know about it. Indeed, he wants others to know exactly how he hurts. Thus he protests and attempts to retaliate, in order to have his tormentor hurt as he hurts. This is the basic source of the lex talionis—an eye for an eye. When I am hurt by you, I want you to hurt as I hurt; therefore, if you hit me, I will hit you back. And it makes no difference that the hitting back doesn't resolve the conflict. This is not a logical process; it is an insistent, impulsive emotional reaction to being hurt.

It is the challenge of society that all human beings become oriented to a principle of operation different from the pleasure principle and the lex talionis. We cannot always have immediate gratification of our desires or impulsively strike back at our frustrations. Our behavior must be regulated for the benefit of everyone. Out of the anarchy of self-centered behavior must come some intelligibly organized existence, with respect for other people and with recognition that some frustrations are inevitable in life and some gratification must be deferred. This principle of operation we call the reality principle.

The important tenet that is derived from this understanding of our beginnings is that while we mature physically and emotionally, the infantile beginning persists in all of us. There is within us all a persisting core of the pleasure principle, a powerful motivating force which is sometimes only slightly covered by a veneer of the reality principle.

A third tenet to assist in our understanding of human behavior is the recognition of the role of the unconscious in our lives. As noted earlier, when an individual is well and healthy, he usually believes that he knows why he does all that he does. Sometimes, however, the explanations for his attitudes and behavior are so shallow that he himself may question their validity. Occasionally, we may admit that we don't know just why we did something or why we have a certain point of view. Understanding human behavior is a complex problem for the average layman who sees a mentally ill person with delusions or hallucinations; he is at a total loss to explain why or how an individual develops such symptoms. The psychiatrist would be, too, without the recognition that there is one part of the individual which seems to be under voluntary control and a larger part which is not under voluntary control. Indeed, there seems to be an unknown, strange, and irrational part of everyone's personality which is much like the hidden part of an iceberg.

By definition, the unconscious is that large region of the mind which is inaccessible to conscious awareness by ordinary means of self-examination or questioning. In this region of our mind are contained the inherited and racial traits and other genetic aspects of our being. Yet beyond these basic, inborn racial traits of mental operation, the unconscious region contains primitive and forbidden strivings, desires which we can openly observe in children but which we must deny as adults. Likewise, this region contains the forgotten incidents of infancy and early childhood, the basic learning experiences which we had during those years.

One cannot prove conclusively that there is an unconscious. Unlike the brain, it cannot be demonstrated as an anatomical unit—although some researchers at the Menninger Foundation have recently found evidence in brain-wave studies of unconscious mental processes. The unconscious is not subject to mathematical proof. Nevertheless, there is a great deal of evidence which points to the existence of some part of the personality which is inaccessible to one's conscious wish or desire either to control or to investigate. That evidence includes observations during hypnosis and sodium amytal interviews, dreams, slips of speech, the lack of recall of memories of childhood experiences, the whole process of forgetting, and the unexplained solution of difficult problems which people have noted after sleeping.

The important point here is that there is a great deal of mental activity which takes place beyond our awareness and which may have a significant role in determining our behavior. It is as if we have within us an "autopilot" which does not always operate in concert with our conscious selves. It is precisely this aspect of the psychodynamic perspective that prompts many people to reject that perspective.

There is some difficulty in coming to grips with some of these formulations because of their abstract nature. However, the difficulty in understanding and dealing with the concepts stems from more than their abstraction. It is intimately related to our self-concept—our idea of just what and who we are and how we operate, our idea of free will. In 1917, Freud forecast that there would be a lot of opposition to some of these concepts, concepts which he was largely responsible for formulating. He knew that they would arouse anxiety and prejudice because they would necessarily wound human self-esteem. In the same way that there is still resistance in some quarters to the evolutionary concepts of Darwin, so there is also a reluctance to accept the idea that the power of the unconscious means that "the Ego is not master in its own house." No one likes to face the fact that he does not know himself as well as he thinks, that he does not control his behavior as fully as he believes, or that he has no real understanding of why he does much of what he does. Freud noted that twice before, mankind had resisted humiliations arising from the development of scientific knowledge—when Darwin demonstrated that man is an animal and when Copernicus proved that the earth is not the center of the universe.

A fourth tenet which is vital to our formulation of the roots of human behavior is an awareness of the process of growth and development and the struggle for identity of the individual. As the infant grows into childhood and adolescence and maturity, he is engaged in a constant process of defining who he is, what he is, and how he is related to the world. While going through the process and learning to master himself and his environment, he has a significant handicap—namely, that he doesn't have the intellectual capacity to understand what is really going on. The infant and the small child don't have the capacity for abstract thinking; this is an ability which is not fully mastered by the normal individual until late adolescence. Without the capacity to conceptualize in abstract terms, a person is forced to interpret what happens to him and around him in the most concrete terms and to relate it to some personal experience. That is, the child cannot really understand concepts like death or religion, or even simpler things like occupations—what Daddy does all day at work. Rather, he must understand these concepts in terms of himself—just as he starts life with a self-centered focus.

Consider, then, some of the major events of infancy and childhood which the developing person must experience, without really understanding why. Put yourself in the place of a child and see how you answer these questions. Why, for instance, should it be necessary to have to use a cold metal instrument to put food in your mouth, when it is so much easier and more comfortable to use one's fingers? Why, if it is so that as an infant one is loved and thought to be of great worth, is a product of that infant or child considered so worthless—that is, why is there such rejection of the first thing we are aware of that is entirely our production, our feces? Why is it so necessary to have to perform the processes of elimination—urination and defecation—in one particular spot? Why does everybody get so upset when you do otherwise? What is so bad about it?

Why, when there is such encouragement for the child to learn to walk and take his first steps, is it then such a crime when he uses this skill to explore the world and gets into things he shouldn't? When the child increases his awareness of the world about him and begins to relate clearly to other people, he inevitably becomes aware that there are two kinds of people. Why? Why is it that some have an anatomy different from the others? Depending upon one's sex, one is then confronted with a most difficult question. As a boy, why did I get it? Why didn't my sisters or my mother get it? Did they once have it and then have it taken away? Could I lose mine? If I am bad, is that what will happen? Et cetera.

Without the capacity really to understand such an abstract concept as sex and the difference of sexes, there must inevitably be some distortions built into the child's explanation for the world about him. And these distortions, coming at the beginning of life experience, may be conceived of in much the same way as the programming of a computer. Once one has an error or a distortion programmed in the computer, it is an extremely difficult process to get it corrected.

Therefore, the process of growth presents some major developmental tasks which stem from the wish to obtain pleasure and satisfaction and gain relief from tensions, both internal and external. These have been variously conceptualized, and one of the important discussions of these tasks has been made by Erik Erikson. He outlined eight ages of man in his **Childhood and Society,** tasks which must be mastered as the child develops into adulthood and establishes a clear identity for himself and a clear interface with his environment.[2] The mastery of these tasks has a lot of bearing on the final capacity of the individual to adjust, and also on the nature of maladjustment.

Erikson characterizes the key issues which face the developing individual at each of his eight stages, and it is in the earliest stages that one finds some of the roots of subsequent disorder. The first task is the problem of basic trust as opposed to basic mistrust and is related to the initial experiences of the infant with those who take care of him—can he count on others to be really concerned about him? Is the world a predictable place? Does it have consistency and continuity to provide some stable base for a developing personality?

Muscular maturation sets the stage for the next task, developing a sense of autonomy and healthy independence, as opposed to experiencing shame, a low self-esteem, and doubt about oneself. This is intimately related to the infant's awareness of his bodily processes and the increasing demands of the parents that he not just "do it" anywhere but learn to control that impulse.

It is the phase of increasing awareness of other people and the differentiation of sexes that prompts the task of developing initiative and a greater freedom to explore and develop oneself, as opposed to a sense of guilt about oneself and a sense of deficiency or a fear of being considered deficient. In the school years, with the entrance into a new life for the child, the task shifts to a sense of industry and application of effort, as opposed to feeling a sense of inferiority and inadequacy in comparison with one's peers. The adolescent struggle, then, is more clearly defined as finding a sense of identity, as opposed to a confusion of one's role in life.

Along the way, the developing personality is learning skills and techniques by which the basic strivings can be achieved and which permit the expression of the impulses in an acceptable manner. Various means of finding pleasure are developed and various objects are utilized in supplying pleasure. At the same time, the individual incorporates, during the course of his growth, internal restrictions. The infant and small child are deterred from misbehaving primarily by the threat of some punishment or the loss of love, which is so important for survival. It is, in other words, simply the external influence that keeps the young child from misbehavior. As the child grows, however, he reaches a stage where he makes the deterrence and restriction a part of his own personality functioning. Guilt is an internal punishment; and as feeling, it develops after the individual has incorporated a conscience, a sense of right and wrong. For the most part, the conscience which is incorporated is parallel to the attitudes of our parents and our teachers and the society in which we live. Thus there are some variations in the nature of the internal policeman in all of us. At the same time, there are some common elements, for we all have had to come to grips with understanding things we couldn't possibly explain at the time—and thus we fall back on magical or simplistic explanations. The world is either good or bad, for or against us when we are children—the world is one and we are the other. This tendency to dichotomize and thereby explain persists in the tendency in later life to view others as for or against us and to see problems strictly in terms of good and bad, black and white.

Personality and Crime

How do all these theoretical formulations provide some understanding of the roots of crime? In general terms, one can recognize that crime is the resolution of a complex struggle for survival of the personality in the environment. It may be seen as a distortion of the adjustment process in which there is a complex resolution of conflict between internal infantile strivings and proscriptions and the external seductions of opportunities for gratification and external restrictions and limitations. The concept is parallel to the resolution of forces formulated in physics. In physics, if several forces are applied to a given point, the resultant movement, in both direction and magnitude, is a function of the interaction and summation of the individual forces. The personality functions in a similar manner, with the resultant action—in this case, crime—being a function of a complex interaction of psychological forces, some of which may be conscious but many more of which may be beyond our awareness.

When we think of crime, we think of anti-social behavior. The typical so-called anti-social personality has two particular defects in its development. First, there is a basic action on impulse, behavior which tends to act at the moment to get immediate satisfaction. Stated differently, there is a poor tolerance for frustration, and at the same time there is usually some impairment of the individual's ability to judge the world about him. He has a poor capacity to test reality and know what he can get away with or what are the appropriate limits for his behavior. In additon, there is commonly poor internal control, or what we might consider little in the way of conscience.

A second feature of the anti-social personality is a focus on oneself, to the exclusion of others. The normal development of the personality involves a stage of narcissism, in which the primary object of gratification is oneself. But in the normal development, the individual learns to get satisfaction from relationships with others and a genuine involvement with others. The anti-social personality has a limited ability to relate to other people in any meaningful manner and is notably shallow in his relationships: manipulating, affectionless, and demanding.

These characteristics are the result of a kind of "hang-up" in the maturational process of the personality, and they are commonly observed in individuals who commit crimes. The usual population of a prison is heavily weighted with persons who present this picture of emotional adjustment. At the same time, there are other patterns of personality functioning in criminals. There are some who appear to be "accidental" criminals or "compulsive" criminals, individuals who do not consciously present themselves as criminals and do not have a self-concept as a criminal. Rather, they seem to be driven into their criminal behavior as a kind of ineffective attempt to get along in life.

Clearly, many criminals operate on the fundamental premise that you have to look out for yourself in life. No one is going to look after you; you can't really count on anyone to be seriously concerned about you. Rather, everyone is out for himself, and you take what you can, when you can. This is but a slight modification of the pleasure principle and its self-reference—and it reflects a breakdown in the initial task of developing a sense of trust in the world.

There are some special problems in the struggle of the adolescent. With a biological resurgence of emotional pressures and the striving for a truly independent and adult identity, the adolescent faces problems in accepting himself as someone distinct and unique in his own right, in maintaining stature among his peers, and in achieving independence from his parents while still maintaining some relationship with them. Indeed, the struggle for independence is an ambivalently sought goal, for what we truly seek is to have our cake and eat it too. We would like to be able to do just what we want when we want to, and at the same time it's nice to be looked after and to have all your needs supplied.

The struggle for independence is no simple process, although we may not be aware of it as such. Sometimes, the only way that we can convince ourselves that we are truly independent and the master of our own decisions is to present a contrast to our parents or the authorities. If we want to be sure that we, rather than our parents, are making our decisions, we can do so by doing something we know our parents would not do. This may be perceived by the parents as a rebellion—whether it is growing long hair or in some other way distinguishing oneself as a unique and separate person.

From the standpoint of society, the rub comes when the rebellion is displaced from the parents to other authorities in society. Further, the developing youngster still has some weaknesses in his reality judgment and in his impulse control, and he is also still learning to gain satisfaction from relationships with others. Juvenile delinquency is thus a manifestation of a wide range of personalities, from the normal to the pathological. The value of the gang is to give strength to the fledgling adult who is seeking independence. When one experiences weakness, one gains strength by union with others, and the gang can serve as a stepping-stone from the dependency of childhood to the independence of adulthood, with the sense of physical and psychological maturity that goes with adulthood.

These are some of the problems and underlying characteristics which affect the nature of the personality in the personality-environment struggle. When we talk of the problems of urban crime, we are then concerned about a particular kind of environment. It is well, therefore, to assess some characteristics of the urban environment which have some bearing on the outcome of the struggle called crime.

Environment: Urban Society

Much has been written about urban problems and the characteristics of urban society. Sociologists have studied the multiple aspects of urban existence in some detail. In their book **The Subculture of Violence,** Wolfgang and Ferracuti note:

> Urban life is commonly characterized by population density, spatial mobility, ethnic and class heterogeneity, reduced family functions, and greater anonymity.[3]

It is well reported that rates for most crimes are highest in the big cities. The President's Commission on Law Enforcement and the Administration of Justice noted that 26 core cities of more than 500,000 people, with less than 18 percent of the total population, account for more than half of all reported index crimes against the person and more than 30 percent of all reported index property crimes.[4] The commission went on to note, however, that it was unable to analyze satisfactorily the factors in the urban settings which would clarify the problems of urban crime. They noted:

> The explanations that have been offered for urban areas having higher rates of crime than rural areas have usually centered around the larger number of criminal opportunities available, a greater likelihood of

association with those who are already criminals, a more impersonal life that offers greater freedom, and in many cases, the harsher conditions of slum life—often in sharp and visible contrast to the affluence of nearby areas. That these factors operate differently with regard to crimes of violence and crimes against property, and with regard to more serious offenses, suggests that the relationship between the rate of crime and the degree of urbanization is a very complicated one.[5]

What is the psychological significance of some of the attributes of the urban setting? One can address this in several ways. First, one can note the particular aspects of more people closer together, with greater heterogeneity, with weaker family ties, and consider this as it affects the struggle of the personality for a unique identity. We referred earlier to the struggle for identity, with the acknowledgment that in the beginning, the "identity" in the mind of the infant is vague and poorly defined. One of the things an infant begins to learn is what his boundaries are—where he stops and others begin.

We postulate that the infant begins with a sense of being everything and being omnipotent. It is as if nothing exists which is not part of the infant. It is thus with some distress that the infant must begin to acknowledge that there is a distinction between himself and the food supply and other sources of satisfaction. It is difficult to give up the sense of security that one might have with omnipotence. At the same time, it can be a relief. To be omnipotent is to have the power to destroy as well as to create—while an immediate impulse might prompt one to destroy, we come to realize that what is destroyed is not easily re-created. This realization is one we struggle with in real life in this atomic age, when we realize that we have within our power the capacity to destroy all and obliterate the work of ages.

As one develops an awareness of having boundaries and not being omnipotent, one goes through a process of developing and revising his Lebensraum, or life space. In our lives we have an extensive mental life, and we allow varying degrees of intrusion into that life. We will expose only so much of our personality, of us, to strangers. We will expose somewhat more to our friends and associates. We will open ourselves yet further to our most intimate relationships, our family. We will allow specialized intrusions for special purposes—if we are sick, we will expose ourselves literally and figuratively to the doctor as we seek help. There is yet an inner core of thoughts and ideas and feelings that we will expose to no one, ideas that would be seen as crazy or sinful. We may express some of these in religious confession, but some we can expose to no one. And there is yet a further level, for in psychiatry we are aware that there are feelings and thoughts that we must hide even from ourselves because they are so unacceptable.

When there is a generous Lebensraum, we may be able to function with many peculiarities and have them go unnoticed. The bizarre behavior of the crank in the smaller community can be tolerated in some ways that might not be possible in the larger urban setting. The contrast, of course, is that in the largest of cities, there is again an opportunity for anonymity which may permit an individual to live with bizarre behavior as long as it doesn't prompt him to run afoul of others. The anxiety that comes when we are forced to tolerate an intrusion into our Lebensraum is of special note, however. A study by a psychiatrist of some of the violent behavior of some prison inmates noted the degree to which the violence was in response to an intrusion into a prisoner's life space. Architects are increasingly aware of some of the spatial needs for the development of emotionally healthy individuals, and it is obvious that increasing urbanization constricts the life space of the individual.

Another way to conceptualize the intrusion into our life space is to compare our existence to the various physical states of the elements: gas, liquid, and solid. As one progresses from the gaseous state to the solid state, there is a greater compression of the atoms, with less tolerance for random motion and greater rigidity in structure. Thus, collisions of the atoms are increasingly frequent. One can get this feeling by riding in the subway during the rush hour.

Beyond the constriction of and the intrusion into our life space, the presence of more people exposes us to more hurts in other ways. There is inevitably a greater awareness that all people are not created equal. Opportunities are not equal—and we are more and more faced with the struggle of maintaining a sense of self-esteem while feeling inferior. An important psychological element which is affected by this experience is the sense of hope that things can be better. As that hope is extinguished, a different life stance can develop, and there is a focus on the narcissistic stance, the stance of self-centeredness.

All these problems are related to our relationships with others. As long as we find that others provide us with more satisfaction and pleasure than disappointment and pain, we will seek to develop relationships outside ourselves. As we experience more pain, we will either withdraw or attack and hurt others in vengeance.

Acknowledging that the issue is very much related to relationships with others, it is not surprising to note the presidential commission's finding that crimes against persons are much greater in urban areas, even taking into consideration the fact that there are more people to be the object of criminal action in cities.

Insofar as urban life, at least in areas of high crime rates (i.e., the low-income, poverty, ghetto areas), is a life of deprivation, one can draw further conclusions as to factors having psychological impact. As the individual grows, in his development there is a seeking for mastery of tasks, which goes hand in hand with a sense of self-worth and goodness. In the mind of the child, goodness is equated with hope and badness with hopelessness. In a setting of deprivation, there are fewer opportunities for the child to demonstrate mastery. Because of the importance of the parental models, there can be even less of a stimulus for the child to develop skills by which the basic impulsive emotional strivings are directed into socially acceptable outlets. For instance, the primary outlet of our aggressive drive in everyday life is in our work. When we are without work, we are therefore forced to seek other outlets for that drive, and if there is no other external activity, like athletics, into which it can be channeled, it may be expressed directly. Or it may be internalized and manifested as depression or illness of some kind. Whether it is expressed outwardly or is internalized is often a function of the behavior of the parental models.

As mentioned earlier, an important element throughout is one's sense of worth, as are the factors in the environment contributing to a positive sense of worth, which is important to sustain, and the factors contributing to a negative sense of worth. Anonymity has been cited as one of the characteristics of the urban environment—at least for many of the inhabitants. Related to anonymity is the sense of being one of many and thus being less in a position to shape one's destiny. This may be stated differently, for such a situation is the complete opposite of the infantile position of omnipotence. If you are truly omnipotent, then you must be extremely careful in what you do. If what you do means nothing, then it doesn't matter what you do. Or you may seek to re-create the position of being powerful and able to affect others. One seeks to be at least equal —and we all know ways of achieving that. One is by using the "great equalizer," the gun.

Increasingly in our society, the individual is getting lost in a maze of numbers and computers and bureaucracy. Lost as individuals, it is not surprising to see individuals unite into groups in order to find some new and identifiable character, and to have a sense of power in determining their future. All too often we find that the good intentions of the welfare services only tend to perpetuate their problem—instead of helping people to make their own destiny, they reinforce their sense of uselessness and hopelessness.

It therefore becomes imperative to keep the value of the individual high, in spite of the population explosion and the complications of modern society. As we restore the worth of the individual, we will find that the need of individuals to seek redemption in groups grows less intense.

The real problem of the urban environment is that it is composed of people. Our greatest pains and hurts in life, from the very beginning, are suffered at the hands of other people, and the major problems in the world are people problems. In work settings, the greatest number of firings occur not because of the inadequacy of individuals to master the technical aspects of their work, but because of their inability to get along with others.

Criminal behavior is thus another manifestation of man's inability to get along with man—which is founded on some basic problems in our growth and development, and a lack of emotional maturation.

Implications

These observations are not intended to serve as answers, but rather to help focus on the important questions we have to face. Understanding a problem is a key first step in problem solving. Once one has carefully identified a problem and defined its nature as objectively as possible, one can then begin to consider what kinds of interventions can be made to alleviate the problem. From my vantage point as a psychiatrist, it is vital to have some awareness of the motivations or the dynamic force which prompts a problem and makes it visible.

In my work in and with various governmental agencies, I am repeatedly aware of the usual approach to problem solving—either to get new legislation or to spend lots of money. There are the vast programs of new housing—the urban renewal efforts, etc. It is impressive how rarely there is any attempt, in the formulation of such programs, to consider the psychological factors. Little does much of the welfare system in this country realize the degree to which it undoes itself psychologically, and instead of fostering new growth of individuals, it only mires them more deeply in a helpless, worthless, social dependency.

The challenge in cities is to help individuals find a new sense of self-worth—and while new housing is one phase of this, just changing the outer structure doesn't change the inner man. Dr. Karl Menninger once observed that you don't need fancy hospital buildings in which to bring about cures of patients—you can cure patients in a barn if you have the right people and the right approach.

When you're dealing with people, two important elements in under-standing are a willingness to listen and an open mind. This is easier said than done, because we just don't respond rationally to problems; we respond emotionally. The ultimate solution to our problems—of crime and the urban situation—is not going to come from the words of one specialist. It must be the result of a group effort, with the integration of the perspectives of several disciplines—law, political science, social sciences, etc.

We have difficulties in dealing with crime and similar problems because we are not immune to the impulses which others have manifested in action. Further, we may be aware of the degree to which we have not yet created the perfect world for ourselves. Individually, we must acknowledge that the place to begin dealing with these problems is within ourselves. We must be a little less self-righteous and sure that we have the right answer. No matter how sophisticated or suave a manner we present to the world, we still have within us childish pressures and reactions. Ultimately, we must acknowledge the fact that the hate in this world can be neutralized effectively only by love, real concern by us for others, which is no less than that which we seek for ourselves.

Notes

1. Karl Menninger, *The Human Mind* (Garden City, Kans.: Garden City Publishing Co., 1930).

2. Erik Erikson, *Childhood and Society* (New York: Norton, 1950).

3. Marvin E. Wolfgang and F. Ferracuti, *The Subculture of Violence* (London: Tavistock, 1967).

4. President's Commission on Law Enforcement and the Administration of Justice, *Crime and Its Impact: An Assessment,* reference report (Washington, D.C.: U.S. Government Printing Office, 1967), p. 28.

5. Ibid., p. 29.

2   Assessing the Current Crime Wave

Albert J. Reiss, Jr.

During the past few years Americans have come to believe that they are being engulfed by a crime wave. In opinion polls, they rank crime as the number one problem of the nation. Indeed, some have even begun to doubt that it is a wave, given the length of time it has been rising. They speak gloomily of moral decay, and of disrespect for the rule of law. The Congress has launched a massive program for law and order in a bill ominously titled The Safe Streets and Omnibus Crime Control Bill.

Clearly, Americans and their legislative representatives are convinced about facts. They regard crime as rising very rapidly. They view with alarm their own safety in the streets and other public places. Many are afraid in their homes. Many believe that the police are hampered in their efforts to control crime and that the courts are not tough enough. All of these are questions of fact. But what are the facts? How much crime is there in American society today? Has there been a change in the crime rate over the past 10 years? How safe are our streets?

Our purpose is to raise some doubts about facts documenting the current crime wave. What we propose to do is to tell you about what recent research on the prevalence and incidence of crime in the United States tells us and what it doesn't tell us. We shall then try to provide a perspective for assessing crime and changes in crime rates.

Let us begin by making what may appear to be an outrageous statement. No matter that the current rate of crime reported in official statistics of crime in the United States by the FBI is believed to be high; in all likelihood it is at least twice as high. In short, we should prepare to accept the idea that the best factual evidence we have today indicates much higher rates of crime in the United States than any official series of statistics report. We propose now to demonstrate that this is the case.

Oddly enough, we shall begin this demonstration by taking the official report of crimes known to the police, as they are summarized and reported in Uniform Crime Reports. Most people are unaware of what is meant by these crime rates. Before discussing these FBI rates, however, we will first indicate some problems posed in measuring crime and developing an index of crime.

Problems in Measurement Posed by an Index of Crime

At first glance, it appears that a single index or measure of the amount of crime in the United States is an important item of information. Just as we measure a death rate, so we may measure a crime rate. Such reasoning rests, nonetheless, on some misconceptions about both death and crime rates.

We shall consider first some misconceptions about the interpretation of simple rates, such as death rates and then turn to crime rates.

Any simple rate for an event consists of but two elements, a population that is exposed to the occurrence of some event (the denominator) and a count of the events (the numerator). Both of these elements are measured for a point or period of time. In calculating a crude death rate, for instance, it is the practice to report the number of deaths for some unit of population, such as every 100 or 1,000 persons, for some unit of time, such as a month or a calendar year. These rates are deliberately termed crude, because we know that within a given period of time not everyone in the population is equally exposed to the risk of death. There are important differences, for example, according to one's age and sex. For that reason, the denominator often is refined into subgroups and a death rate is calculated separately for each subgroup. These are generally termed specific rates; the death rate for a particular race, age, and sex subgroup—say Negro women, aged 20-24—is a race-age-sex specific death rate.

Though such crude and specific rates are useful for some purposes, they are limited both for an analysis of the causes of death and as a basis for public policies about how to reduce the death rate. The main reason for this limitation is that we know people die from many different causes. Death from an automobile accident is quite different from death due to lung cancer. Obviously public policy when one tries to reduce the death rate due to factors connected with driving automobiles will be quite different from when it has some relationship to lung cancer, such as smoking. To go one step further, we have learned a great deal scientifically about causes of death by classifying types of death and searching for their causes. When one has some understanding of death from a particular cause, one may calculate a separate rate for deaths from that cause. Ever since developing evidence of a strong relationship between smoking and disease, we have calculated a death rate for diseases to which smoking is causally related, including cancer of the lung, larynx, and lip, and chronic bronchitis.[1]

The analogy to crime should be clear. We know that crime is not unitary, nor are causes the same for all types of crime. What causes most types of crime is not clear, but that they have single common causes that affect their incidence seems doubtful. Even in the absence of causal knowledge, we know that policies and practices for crime control differ considerably, depending upon the conditions under which types of crime occur. A policy to control auto theft can be very different from one to control aggravated assault. A simple crime rate, therefore, is of little use either for causal analysis or for public policy.

The analogy between death and crime rates should not be overdrawn, lest it lead to further misconceptions. Some of these differences merit attention because they should influence our choice of social indicators for crime.

First, death is an event that occurs for every member of the population; but every member of the population is not a victim of a crime. In addition, some persons can never be a victim of certain types of crime; men cannot be raped or have their purse snatched, for example. Second, death can occur only once for any member of the population, while crime, like illness or accident, can occur repeatedly. For such events both multiple victimization and multiple offenses are possible. There is, third, the fact that crime is a relational phenomenon—between victims and offenders. One therefore can calculate offense, victim, offender, and/or victim-offender rates. Indeed, a crime may involve a single victim, several victims, an organization, or even a diffuse public. Furthermore, the exposed population is not always made up of persons. It can consist of organizations such as businesses, or even the general public, as in offenses against public order. Fourth, an offender can commit several crimes at the same point in time. An offender may assault the owner of an automobile and steal his car and the possessions that are in it. He can be charged with assault and two counts of larceny. Fifth, the relative absence of completeness in registration of offenses, offenders, and victims makes difficult the interpretation of changes in rates. With present systems for gathering and processing information on crimes, we lack the knowledge that would permit us to separate any actual increase from any registration increase.

Finally, for many classes of crimes, unlike most classes of death, it is important to know where the crime occurred as well as where the victim resides. The failure to separate place of occurrence from place of residence of victim makes for difficulties in interpreting rates based on an exposed population of residents for any given jurisdiction in the United States. This problem arises from the way data are processed in police registration systems.

It should be evident, therefore, that any simple crime rate, unlike a death rate, lacks the specification necessary for reasonable interpretation. The problem therefore becomes one of deciding what kinds of rates it makes sense to calculate, given our current knowledge of the causes of crime, the situations under which crimes occur, our aims in public information, our goals in the formation of public policy to deal with crime, and our goals in the development of organizational strategies to reduce crime.

Criteria for Measuring Crime

More rational ways that crime may be measured than those now in use are possible. We propose three such criteria for a crime rate: (1) that the information in the rate count the crime events only for a population that could be exposed to that crime; (2) that the choice of the rate be appropriate to organized means for gathering it; (3) that the information from the rate permit potential victims, whether persons or organizations, to calculate their chances of victimization more rationally. These are commonly called crime victimization rates, though they are rarely calculated.

Even the official reporting of crime today is highly selective. We lack information, for the most part, on many white-collar crimes, such as fraud, and on much organized crime. For many misdemeanors and minor offenses, it is generally agreed that many of these crimes go unreported. We therefore shall limit discussion primarily to what the FBI defines as major or index crimes—those that it uses to construct its crime index to measure changes in crime in the United States. These include only criminal homicide, forcible rape, robbery, aggravated assault, larceny over $50, and auto theft. On these crimes hinges the public's information about crime in the United States.

Considering only these offenses, there are many problems in their enumeration and in selecting an exposed population as a base for a crime rate. Not all of these problems are dealt with in what follows, but it should be evident from the illustrations that our current information makes it difficult to construct a highly valid and reliable rate.

For those unfamiliar with the Uniform Crime Reporting System, several important features should be understood before considering specific rates based on them. First, each crime or attempted crime is counted in only one crime classification. When several different major, or Part I, offenses are committed by a person or group at the same time, the offense is classified in the highest-ranking offense in the rank order of Part I offenses: criminal homicide, forcible rape, robbery, assault, burglary, larceny-theft, and auto theft. Thus, a crime involving the murder of a rape victim is classified as a criminal homicide, not as both a rape and a homicide. Legally an offender could be charged with both offenses.

Second, the number of offenses counted in any criminal event is classified differently for crimes against persons and crimes against property. For offenses against the person, the number of offenses counted is the number of persons unlawfully killed, raped, maimed, wounded, or assaulted, plus any attempts to do so. For offenses against property, an offense is counted only for each distinct operation or attempt. The criterion "operation" relates to a crime incident; hence, if 20 people are robbed in a tavern, it is counted as one offense, not 20. The distinction between crimes against persons and crimes against property is not a distinction between persons as victims and housholds or organizations as victims, since persons are victims when their property is taken.

Third, it should be clear that a distinction is made between the complaint or report of an offense and its bona fide status. The number of offenses reported or known to the police differs from the number of actual offenses reported, in that the latter count results when the former is reduced by the number of false or baseless complaints, as determined from department rules for "unfounding" a complaint.

Finally, there are problems in classifying crimes arising from the organized ways police have for knowing when events that are classified as crimes occur. The main ways they have for knowing them are by responses to citizen complaints that such an event is in progress or has occurred or by some police strategy for gathering intelligence on events that potentially might be crimes, such as by routine patrol or detective work.

A little reflection on what comes to the police as complaints or even as observations by police officers readily suggests that the problem of determining whether an event is to be classified as a crime depends upon the nature of the information received. Generally the police must evaluate information initially received from citizens by investigating whether or not the complaint constitutes a crime event. Obviously both officer discretion or judgment and departmental criteria affect the classification of such an event as a crime. But citizen reports do not present a homogeneous set of events where the same criteria can readily be applied to determine whether or not the event has occurred. This is particularly so for the criteria to judge whether or not the event actually occurred.

The problem of knowing whether an event has occurred is especially difficult when the determination depends upon the status of the complainant, of witnesses, or of offenders. Some offenses are known to the police only through an arrest situation where the offender is present. This is particularly true for offenses involving morals or violations of moral codes. Thus, the police do not usually know about crimes of drunkenness except through the arrest of persons who are called drunks. One clearly cannot have an offense of resisting arrest without some person under arrest engaging in resisting behavior. On the other hand, crimes against property can be known to the police even though no offender is known. Events of shoplifting can be determined only by observation; this is much less likely to be the case for burglary, where evidence of entry, etc., makes determination less difficult. Offenses against the public peace and order occur only when there is a complainant present, while burglary can occur without the presence of a complainant. Some offenses have only testimony or behavior as evidence, while for others there is physical evidence.

Given the diversity of sources and types of information on crimes, the procedures one has for determining whether a crime has occurred must vary. It is doubtful, therefore, whether it makes much logical sense to compute an overall measure of crime, if by that is meant a measure of whether events have occurred. Crime in that sense is unlike births or deaths, where the event is more clearly specified. It is much more like illness, where the organized procedures of medicine are the major basis for knowing and classifying illness. Subjective accounts of either illness or crime by complainants pose problems of validity. So do professional determinations where the procedures rest largely on accounts or judgment rather than on observation or means of measurement. Much of the difficulty in crime reporting, like that in illness reporting, arises from our present procedures of "diagnosing" events that come to our attention.

The Crime Index

The Uniform Crime Reporting Program uses seven crime classifications to measure the trend and distribution of crime in the United States. These crimes are those of murder or criminal homicide, forcible rape, robbery, aggravated assault, burglary, larceny of $50 and over in value, and auto theft. Basically they were selected to make up the index because they are regarded as the major crimes against persons and their property.

When one reads that the crime index has risen, what does this mean? How significant is any crime in contributing to a rise in value in this index? Three crimes (burglary, larceny over $50 in value, and auto theft) normally account for more than 85 percent of all crime that makes up the index. They are the major crimes against property, not persons. In 1968, for example, these three crimes accounted for 87 percent of the crimes in the index. Burglary accounted for 42 percent; larceny over $50 for 28 percent; and auto theft for 17 percent.[2] It can easily be shown that any rise in the crime index from year to year is largely affected, therefore, by changes in the reporting of crimes against property, a matter we shall return to later.

Of the remaining four crimes, only two are of any additional significance in the crime index—aggravated assaults and robbery. In 1968, aggravated assault and robbery each accounted for 6 percent of all crime that makes up the index.[3] Even here it can be seen that a rise in the robbery rate would have a negligible effect on the index, as, say, compared with a comparable rise in the burglary rate. For every robbery reported, there are more than eight burglaries reported. Finally, forcible rape, with 0.7 percent in 1968, and criminal homicide, with 0.3 percent can be seen as contributing little to any change in the index. In short, major crimes against the person are a relatively small part of the crime index. They accounted for but 13 percent of all index crime in 1968.[4]

Looking at one's chances of being a victim of a crime as a person as compared with being a victim through property loss, the chances are less than one in five that one will be victimized as a person for one of these major crimes. We now propose to show that even such calculations can be quite misleading.

Victimization Rates for UCR Reports

Let us return now to the problem of providing victimization rates for our current crime statistics and a demonstration that victimization rates are much higher than reported crime rates. For the seven major offenses in the Uniform Crime Index, it should be clear that the exposed or potential victim population is not the same for all of these types of crime. Anyone can be killed or assaulted. A person or a business can be robbed. Only women can be raped. Only dwelling units, businesses, or other organizations can be burglarized. Only automobile owners can have an auto stolen. Few children can be victims of larceny of $50. What is more, some types of larceny, should one be interested in them, refer only to some group, such as pocket-picking to men and purse-snatching to women. Yet the Uniform Crime Reporting system calculates crime rates using every man, woman, and child in the United States as a base for the rate.

It is reasonable, then, to propose that a population which risks crime (the population exposed to victimization) be selected according to the type of offense and the status of the victim in the offense for purposes of calculating crime rates. Quite clearly, where the exposed population is the number of organizations, such rates may be quite different in size from those that would be obtained were the general population of persons used as the base for calculating the rate. This will be evident in the examples below.

Forcible Rape

Forcible rape is one of the major crimes in the UCR Index for which a rate is calculated. The reported rape rate for the United States, or for any city such as Philadelphia, is based on the population of every man, woman, and child resident in the United States. For 1968, the rape rate was 1.6 for every 10,000 inhabitants. (See Table 1.)

Table 1

Rates of Forcible Rape for Selected Exposed Civilian Resident
Populations, United States: 1965 and 1968.

Exposed population	Year	Total number of persons	Rapes known to police	Rate per 10,000	Ratio of rapes to women
Civilian residents	1968	199,861,000	31,060	1.6	1:6,435
	1965	193,818,000	22,467	1.2	1:8,627
All females	1968	102,291,000	31,060	3.0	1:3,293
	1965	98,704,000	22,467	2.3	1:4,394
Females 14 and over	1968	74,932,000	31,060	4.1	1:2,412
	1965	71,052,000	22,467	3.2	1:3,161

Source: U.S. Bureau of the Census, *Population Estimates,* Current Population Reports, Series P-25, No. 416, Table 2; *Crime in the United States, Uniform Crime Reports: 1965* and *1968* (Washington, D.C.: U.S. Department of Justice, Federal Bureau of Investigation, 1966 and 1969.)

There may be some use in knowing that there were 1.6 forcible rapes or attempts for every 10,000 inhabitants in the United States in 1968, even though by definition only women can be victims of rape. Generally, however, our police are more interested in the question of how many total rapes there were and where they occurred, since that defines their prevention and control problem. As citizens, we are more interested in the chances of victimization for women.

What was the victimization rape rate for 1968, the last year for which a report is available from the FBI? Considering only all women as the population risking rape, the rape rate in 1968 was a little more than double that reported, a not unexpected result, since women are slightly in the majority in the United States. One in every 3,293 women in the United States in 1968 risked rape, assuming no victims of multiple rape.

But let us go a step further. While there are occasional forcible rapes of women under 14 years of age, their number is very small—so small, in fact, as to have only a negligible effect on the overall rape rate. When one calculates the rape rate for all women 14 years of age and over, it turns out to be 4.1 per 10,000 women, or one in every 2,412 women 14 years and older risked being the victim of a forcible rape. (See Table 1.) Thus, realistically, women in the United States had close to a three times greater chance of being raped than that officially reported for the United States.

These are rates for the United States. Clearly the probability of victimization varies considerably by place of residence and even within places such as cities. Just one illustration of how much difference there can be by place of residence. We have calculated the rape rate for the city of Chicago for 1965. The rape rate for women 14 years of age and over in Chicago in 1965 was 9.1 per 10,000. A woman in Chicago thus had a chance of one in 1,100 in 1965 of being raped, assuming no repeated victimization during the year. Need one add that such chances were much higher than the officially reported one for every 3,161 men, women, and children for that year.

What should be obvious is that current practices of reporting rates of forcible rape for all residents grossly understate the probability of victimization by rape. Indeed, even the rates reported here are less refined than they should or could be, were we to make some slight changes in our reporting system. We know that victims of rape are more likely to be young women than older women, for example. Clearly, the chances that a young woman in Chicago will be raped are quite high—much less than one in 1,000 in 1965. In some areas of the city of Chicago, it may be as high as one in 100.

Robbery

Robbery is a form of theft where the offender uses force or violence to obtain property from a victim or obtains property from the victim by use of threats, weapons, or other means. According to UCR for 1968, the robbery rate was 131 per 100,000 population in the United States, or one robbery for every 763 persons.[5]

Robbery is primarily a crime against city dwellers and businesses, however. In 1968, the 56 major metropolitan cities in the United States with 250,000 or more inhabitants accounted for 74 percent of all robberies. For 1968, the officially reported robbery rate per 100,000 was 433 for cities with more than 250,000 inhabitants, 45 for suburban areas, and only 13 for all other sections.[6]

Although a person is in some sense the victim of a robbery, in that all robberies involve a person, the loss is not always sustained by a person. The largest proportion, 58 percent, of all 1968 robberies in the 684 cities with 25,000 or more inhabitants occurred on highways or public ways. Many of these involve businesses, since a very substantial proportion of all robberies are against transportation agencies, with bus and cab drivers the immediate victims. In 1968, 29 percent of all robberies were against businesses, in that they occurred within business settings. Assuming that of the 180,722 robberies reported for these 684 cities, 52,553, or 29 percent, were against businesses,[7] the rate is substantially higher than the 131 reported for all inhabitants. For an estimated 3.5 million employing establishments in the United States in 1968, the robbery rate would be 1,501 per 100,000 establishments, or more than 11 times that for inhabitants. Clearly the likelihood of a business being robbed is much greater than that reported.

During 1968 a sample survey of all United States businesses by the Small Business Administration obtained information on all crimes against businesses, whether they were reported to the police or not. Using business establishments as the risk population, we found that roughly one in every 20 businesses was robbed during the previous year. But the rate was much greater for businesses located in ghetto areas. More than one in five ghetto businesses (23 per 100) reported a robbery the previous year.[8] Clearly the risk of robbery is much higher for all businesses than that obtained from our official statistics.

Burglary

When a person unlawfully enters a dwelling unit, commercial establishment, or any other building or structure to steal or commit any felony, it is considered burglary. It should be clear from this definition that while the victims of burglary are one or more persons—the owners—the unit to which burglary attaches is some structure—a public building, a residence, a commercial house, or any structure attached to a property, such as a garage. Generally persons are not present when burglaries occur. From the standpoint of the problems of policing and of citizens, the logical question would appear to be, what is the likelihood that some residence or establishment I own or rent will be burglarized?

In 1968 the burglary rate reported for the United States was 109 per 10,000 inhabitants, or one burglary for every 91 inhabitants. (See Table 2.) When we calculate burglary rates separately for dwelling units (residences) and business establishments (see Table 2), the risks change considerably. Thus, one in every 60 residences was burglarized in 1968, assuming no multiple burglaries during the year—a not altogether reasonable assumption, since multiple burglaries occur. For business establish-

Table 2

Burglary Rates by Type of Burglary, United States, 1965 and 1968

Type of burglary	Year	Number of inhabitants, households, or establishments	Number of burglaries	Rate per 10,000	Ratio of burglaries to inhabitants/ households/ establishments
Total index	1968	199,861,000	1,828,900	91	1:109
	1965	193,818,000	1,173,201	60	1:165
Residence	1968	58,845,000	982,119	166	1: 60
	1965	57,251,000	580,735	101	1: 98
Night	1968		448,080	76	1:131
	1965		297,993	52	1:192
Day	1968		534,039	90	1:110
	1965		282,742	49	1:202
Nonresidence	1968	3,500,000	846,781	2,419	1: 4
	1965	3,384,398	592,466	1,750	1: 6
Night	1968		738,876	2,111	1: 5
	1965		538,499	1,591	1: 6
Day	1968		107,905	308	1: 32
	1965		53,967	159	1: 62

Sources: *Crime in the United States, Uniform Crime Reports: 1965* and *1968* (Washington, D.C.: U.S. Department of Justice, Federal Bureau of Investigation, 1966 and 1969) Table 14 in the *Reports* provides a percentage distribution for burglaries in 646 cities 25,000 and over — this distribution is applied to the burglary total in Table 1 of the *Reports* to provide estimates for total U.S. burglaries; U.S. Bureau of the Census, *Population Estimates,* Current Population Reports, Series P-25, Table 2, total resident population, all ages; *Households and Families by Type,* Current Population Reports, Series P-20 (July 1965; 1968); *1965 and 1967 County Business Patterns,* Table 2.

ments the figures are more startling, however; one in every four business establishments in the United States risked a burglary in 1968, assuming no multiple burglaries. For households there is not much difference by day or night, while for businesses the risk is far greater at night, a not surprising finding, given the presence of persons on business premises during the day. Clearly, when risks are calculated for owners, renters, or occupants, the risk is much greater than that reported in our official statistics.

Table 3

Auto Theft Rates, United States, 1960, 1965, and 1968

Year	Number of auto thefts	Number of inhabi- tants	Rate per 10,000 popula- tion	Number of motor ve- hicle re- gistrations	Rate per 10,000 regis- trations	Ratio of cars stolen to auto regis- trations
1960	318,500	179,992,000	18	73,877,000	43	1:232
1965	486,568	193,818,000	25	90,357,000	54	1:186
1968	777,755	199,861,000	39	101,039,000	76	1:149

Sources: *Crime in the United States, Uniform Crime Reports: 1960, 1965,* and *1968* (Washington, D.C.: U.S. Government Printing Office, 1961, 1966, and 1969), Table 1; U.S. Bureau of the Census, *Population Estimates,* Current Populations Reports, Series P-25; U.S. Bureau of Public Roads, *Statistical Summary.*

Auto Theft

One other example, the case of auto theft, may serve to show how risks are much higher when one changes the exposed population to a more logical base of risk. Each theft or attempted theft of a motor vehicle is counted as an offense. The UCR system calculates auto theft rates for every 100,000 inhabitants, though many of these persons are not even of an age to drive, much less own, an automobile. Logically, only owners can be victims of auto theft. For that reason we used motor vehicle registrations rather than people for the risk population for auto theft. (See Table 3.) For 1968, the official auto theft rate was 39 for every 10,000 inhabitants, but it is almost double that for every 10,000 automobile registrations: 76. The ratio of cars stolen to registrations was, in fact, one stolen for every 130 automobile registrations in the United States. Again, it is evident that one's risk as an automobile owner is much higher than that shown in our official statistics for inhabitants.

Thus, victim-oriented statistics show much higher rates than do our present official statistics. For major offenses considered, the rates are more than twice those reported. For some classes of risks, such as businesses, they are generally far greater. Our sense of how much crime there is from the victim point of view should be that it is much higher than we officially recognize.

The Dark Figure of Crime

Yet we know that much crime goes unreported. Recent sample surveys for the National Crime Commission and the Small Business Administration demonstrate that much major crime goes unreported. Just how much serious crime does go unreported by citizens? The National Opinion Research Center study of a sample of U.S. citizens showed that in 1965 more than half of all crimes and 38 percent of all UCR Index crimes went unreported to the police. Sample surveys in high crime rate areas of Boston, Chicago, and Washington, D.C., generally showed even higher rates of underreporting of major crimes. For the eight precincts combined in these cities, the survey estimates for index offenses was four times that of the rates known to the police in these cities.[9] There was considerable evidence in the surveys that these estimates are actually conservative ones. There is good reason to believe that one's chances of victimization from major crimes are even greater.

What emerges, then, from an examination of both official statistics and from our sample survey studies is the clear picture that we live with far more major crime than that reported in official statistics.

Naturally one wants to raise the question of why so much crime should go unreported. Sample surveys provide some general answers to this question. For crimes against property, one of the major reasons for non-reporting derives from the insurance of property. Insurance leads both to high reporting by some sectors of the population and to low reporting by others. Many persons and businesses without insurance fail to report crimes against property because they see little to be gained personally from such reporting. They cannot make an insurance claim. Correlatively, insured persons or businesses are more likely to report such crimes unless —and this is important—they are reporting for a home or business in a high crime rate area, and most particularly if they have previously made an insurance claim. The reason for this is fairly obvious. They do not wish to take the risk of having their insurance policy canceled or of having their insurance premium rise because their risk is higher. Hence, many do not report crimes against their property because they are afraid they then would not be covered for the really big claim or that their insurance costs will be so high they cannot afford them.

But these are not the only reasons and certainly do not cover under-reporting of major crimes against the person. About one in three citizens in the Washington, D.C., studies of victimization by crime said they did not report the crime because they felt nothing could be done about it.[10] Generally, they take a negative, though perhaps not altogether unrealistic, view of the crime-solving process. They know that most such crimes will go unsolved, and for many, as already noted, there is no personal gain from reporting a crime. The second major reason indicated negative attitudes toward the police—they do not want to get involved with the police because they fear or dislike them, or have little confidence in them to do anything about their crime. About 3 percent feared reprisal if they reported the crime. Other reasons relate to unwillingness to get involved with anyone, seemingly, in many cases, because it was seen as a time-consuming process, again with no net gain to the person reporting.

There is little doubt, then, that a substantial proportion of the citizenry anticipates no personal gain in reporting crimes against them or their property. Some of their unwillingness no doubt relates to their images of the police; much of it, perhaps, because they see either no gain or even an actual loss—such as insurance cancellation or reprisal—if they do report the crime to the police. Such underreporting poses major problems of citizen cooperation and new institutional arrangements if we are to derive a more valid statement of the crime problem in the United States.

Is the Crime Rate Rising?

What should now be clear is that neither absolute official crime statistics nor the statistics derived from them are easily interpretable to members of the public. How can the public interpret easily whether the absolute number is large or small and the chances of victimization, given present methods of crime reporting? But an even more difficult question is how anyone can decide whether the crime rate is rising or falling. It is to this problem that we now turn.

What has been presented up to now should cause some real concern as to whether we can tell whether the crime rate rises or falls. Only two facts are established from what we presently know about crime: (1) the official police statistics on crime show increasing numbers of crime each year and, relative to total population, the rate is going up; (2) there is much crime, including index crimes, that goes unreported to the police.

A first major reason, then, why we cannot tell whether the crime rate is rising or falling is the fact that so much crime goes unreported to the police. Anything that will increase either police reporting or police intervention to detect more crimes should increase the amount of crime officially known to the police. In short, official statistics can constantly dip into the dark figure of crime.

Are there reasons to believe that more crime is being made known to the police each year? The answer clearly is yes. Let us explore some of those reasons.

First, we have good reason to believe that police departments are better equipped to receive, record, and process crimes. The upgrading of police technology and greater control of the processing of crime information means there is more crime officially known to the police. Several major changes contribute to this. With centralized communication systems, citizen reporting to the police is made easier. At the same time, it is more difficult for local police commanders to "kill" crimes in their district by not reporting them. Furthermore, the increased use of radio dispatching and an attempt to handle all calls for police assistance undoubtedly add to the official figures. My point is very simply that the better police departments become, the more crime will be known to the police without any actual increase in crime because of reduction of the dark figure of crime—that which occurs but is not presently reported or known to them.

Second, there is good reason to believe that citizens are now more likely to mobilize the police than they have been in years past. Perhaps there are many reasons for this, including the likelihood that when citizens perceive that crime is a major problem, they are more likely to report crimes against themselves. But one of the most important reasons perhaps derives from the changing relationship of Negroes to the police.

We know that at least in many large cities Negroes contribute disproportionally to the increase in the crime rate. But this probably is due largely to two things. First, Negroes are increasingly willing to call the police for assistance, since they are more likely to get such assistance as the police department increases its services to them and becomes more ready to treat their calls as crime matters. Closely related to this is a second reason. Blacks today believe it is their right to be treated with equality and appear to be exercising the right in many ways, including an insistence that police pay attention to crimes against them. In short, there is a minor kind of revolution in which ghetto populations are much more likely today than even a few years ago to report crimes against themselves.

A third major reason for the growing crime rate undoubtedly is the growing insurance industry, and most particularly the advent of the homeowner's policy and automobile insurance policies. This could account in large measure for much of the actual increase in reporting crimes against property. Making an insurance claim generally means that the company will insist that the crime have been reported to the police; at least most citizens believe that to be true. Hence, if one anticipates making an insurance claim, one reports the crime. This factor alone could account for much of the increases in crimes against the property of the so-called propertied classes.

There are several other reasons why we have difficulty in knowing whether the crime rate is rising. These deal with problems in the measurement of crime and the statistics used.

First, we know that crimes are more likely to be committed by young people than older people. We know at the same time that our population bulks heaviest in the younger age group. Some of the rise in crime, then, is due simply to the fact that we now have more young people each year in the crime-prone ages. It has been shown that some of the increase in the crime rate is a function of this changing age composition. Overall rates can be expected to increase or decrease as our age structure changes.

For some crimes, the increase may be due solely to changes that are underway in the society. One such change is secular inflation in the cost of goods. This inflation affects particularly the category of larcenies of $50 and over. Each year many items that are stolen the previous year fall into the category of larceny over $50 simply because goods cost more. Consider only one category. Whereas some years ago any bicycle stolen was a larceny of less than $50, today many bicycles cost more than that. To be sure, economies of scale may also reduce the price of some commodities. What is clear is that we now do not know how much of an increase in the larceny rate may be due to such factors related to the cost of goods.

Closely related to changes in the actual value of goods is police practice in determining the value of goods. There are no uniform national practices for determining the value of goods stolen. Many police departments, in fact, depend upon a citizen's estimate. There is some good reason to believe that not only do citizens increasingly overreport such values for insurance purposes but that they are the mechanism for reporting inflationary prices.

But are there changes that might lead to an actual increase in crime, so that we might say there has been some "upsurge" of crime in this country? Such a question is not easily answered without the careful monitoring of both unreported and reported crimes. The question must even be redefined in some way, since any answer to the question of how much crime there is depends upon some organized means of knowing, each of which has genuine problems of validity and reliability.[11]

Apart from any precise answer, is there reason to conclude that the crime rate may be rising? To answer that question, one should have good causal theory about what causes crime and then see whether there have been marked changes in the causal factors that might lead to an increase in crime.

Can we say much about changes in such causes? One thing is clear, given the rapid increase in crime—officially documented by the FBI as an 89 percent rise in index crimes from 1960 to 1967[12]—we would have to look to some very substantial changes to make the crime rate rise that fast in so short a period of time, changes that occurred during this period of time or during some earlier period that the present crime-producing cohorts experienced. Short of that, it would have to rest in some particular relationship among smaller changes that have suddenly produced a sharp increase.

We are then forced to conclude that no current theory of crime would account very well for such a sharp increase. Therefore, much of the increase must be due to factors already mentioned. Briefly, we are a society that has a much higher rate of crime than what is officially known to the police; our crime rate rises and falls according to how citizens and the police treat matters as crimes for official attention.

Is there no reason, then, to conclude that the crime rate has been rising, given the fact that many citizens and the police have a strong sense that it is rising? Mention has already been made of the fact that some of the increase in crime is due to our changing age structure. What that says is that assuming there were no changes in what causes crime among the young, we still would have more crime because we have more young.

What may have changed, however, are the opportunities to commit crime and the mobility of persons to take advantage of these opportunities. The argument runs something like this: Americans today are more careless about their possessions and property because they have more of them. They leave auto and house doors unlocked, purses lying around, bicycles unlocked, and so on. These practices create more opportunities for crime. At the same time, Americans of all kinds are freer to move about unquestioned and unhampered by either public or police restrictions. They are in a better position to commit crimes, whether by being freer in public places or by moving more freely to private places. Such freedom may also include greater aggression toward one another, since contact is increased and restraint is decreased.

While it is conceivable that these changes in affluence and in mobility of persons may account for an increase in crime, it is doubtful that they are powerful enough to account for the large changes from year to year.

Thus, it seems doubtful that such changes could account for the reported 16 percent increase in major crimes between 1966 and 1967.[13]

Changes in Our Sense of Crime

Yet, we have already said that both the public and the police sense that crime has increased. We know from our studies that many citizens fear crime. In four high crime rate police precincts we surveyed in Boston and Chicago, 20 percent of the citizens wanted to move because of their fear of crime.[14] What is more, many citizens have taken steps to protect themselves from what they see as a rise in crime. Six of every 10 residents in the high crime rate areas of Boston and Chicago took steps to protect themselves from crime: 50 percent of all residents stay off the streets at night, for example.[15] In the national survey for the National Crime Commission 37 percent said they kept firearms in the house for protection.[16] What is more to the point, almost six of every 10 citizens in the high crime rate areas of Boston and Chicago believe there is more violent crime in their city in recent years.[17] Clearly, people's sense of crime is high, and they regard it as rising.

Might there be reasons why people regard crime as rising even though the actual rise is much less than that which appears? Of course. The fact that people are told crime is rising should convince people that it is true.

Some things about crime appear to have changed. For one thing, its occurrence seems less confined in our cities than formerly. There are areas of Chicago, Philadelphia, New York, Boston, Washington, D.C., or any other major U.S. city where one formerly could walk with reasonable safety but where now the level of crime is such that it appears unwise. One factor may be that as more and more citizens flee to the suburbs—and that flight is very rapid from many cities that have had a large influx of Negroes—less and less of the central city becomes a low crime rate area. Indeed, if one thinks of that area as increasing in a constant ratio to the expansion at the periphery, the expansion of the high crime rate area would be considerable over so short a period as 10 years. One senses that in cities like Detroit, Chicago, and Washington, D.C., for example, where the influx of low-income persons has been very high over the past decades, the unsafe area is larger than in cities like Los Angeles or San Francisco.

Put in another way, there is no good reason to assume that as cities grow, the high crime rate area should remain fixed geographically. There is every reason to assume it will not. Hence, the unsafe area of a city must grow if the city continues to grow. Much research needs to be done to document whether such changes have indeed been taking place.

Epilogue

We have tried to say several things. First, we have tried to say that we have a false sense of crime in America. We have both a higher rate of crime than any official statistics disclose because of much unreported crime and a higher rate of victimization because of the way we calculate our statistics on crime.

Second, we have tried to say that much of the reported increase in crime may be solely a product of dipping into the dark figure of unreported crime.

Third, we have tried to say that we have no causal theory that would explain such a rapid rise in crime as officially reported for the past seven years. This makes it even more likely that the increase is overestimated.

Fourth, we have suggested that some changes may account for an actual increase in crime, particularly an increase in the opportunities to commit crimes and the greater mobility of people to commit them.

Finally, recognizing that many Americans perceive crime to be rising, we have suggested that some of this may be due to the media portrayal of crime, and some may be a consequence of the fact that as our cities grow, the areas that are unsafe must also grow, even with no overall change in the rate of crime.

How much crime is there? Much more than most Americans know. Has it increased? We cannot say with any degree of certainty. Much may be, and probably is, due to changes in how we report and measure crime.

Notes

1.   National Center for Health Statistics, *Mortality from Diseases Associated with Smoking: United States, 1950-64,* Series 20, No. 4 (Washington, D.C.: U.S. Government Printing Office, 1966), pp. 2-9.

2.   *Crime in the United States: Uniform Crime Reports, 1968* (Washington, D.C.: U.S. Government Printing Office, 1969), Table 1, p. 58.

3.   Ibid.

4.   Ibid.

5.   Ibid.

6.   Ibid., Table 9, p. 96.

7.   Ibid., Table 18, p. 107.

8.   Albert J. Reiss, Jr., *Field Survey of Crime Against Small Business,* A Report of the Small Business Administration Transmitted to the Select Committee on Small Business, U.S. Senate, 91st Cong., 1st sess., Document No. 91-14, April 3, 1969, pp. 76-77.

9.   Albert D. Biderman, "Surveys of Population Samples for Estimating Crime Incidence," *Annals of the American Academy of Political and Social Science,* CCCLXXIV (November, 1967), 16-33.

10. *Report on a Pilot Study in the District of Columbia on Victimization and Attitudes Toward Law Enforcement,* Field Surveys, I, A Report of a Research

Submitted to the President's Commission on Law Enforcement and the Administration of Justice (Washington, D.C., U.S. Government Printing Office, 1967), pp. 153-154.

11.   See Albert D. Biderman and Albert J. Reiss, Jr., "On Exploring the Dark Figure of Crime," *Annals of the American Academy of Political and Social Science,* CCCLXXIV (November, 1967), 1-15.

12.   *Crime in the United States,* p. 2.

13.   Ibid.

14.   *Studies in Crime and Law Enforcement in Major Metropolitan Areas,* Field Surveys, III, Vol. 1, A Report of Research Submitted to the President's Commission on Law Enforcement and the Administration of Justice (Washington, D.C.: U.S. Government Printing Office), p. 31.

15.   Ibid., pp. 97-98.

16.   President's Commission on Law Enforcement and the Administration of Justice, *The Challenge of Crime in A Free Society* (Washington, D.C., U.S. Government Printing Office, 1967), p. 20.

17.   Ibid.

3   The Social Cost of Crime and Crime Prevention

Simon Rottenberg

Criminal behavior is costly to society mainly because it afflicts and causes harm. Its implications and the appropriate treatment can be more easily discerned if it is thought of in the context of other classes of harm that occur in society.

A partial catalogue of harmful behavior includes the following cases:

1. In competition some are more skillful and shrewd than others. If buyers of shoes can opt among a number of shoe-selling shops that compete for their patronage, some shops will survive and others go under. The superiority of the skills of the winners does harm to the losers.

2. Constraints on competition harm those who are relatively disadvantaged by the rules of the constraining game. If seniority systems rank-order workers in the rationing of preferential employments, some will be at the end of the queue. They suffer for the gains of those that the rules put at the queue's head.

3. The use of resources for any purpose forestalls their use for other purposes. Land on which a commercial office structure is built cannot be a site for residential housing. Those with strong preference for the consumption of housing services are outbid. They are harmed because the price of housing will be higher than would otherwise be true.

4. Discovery and innovation diminish the value of some capital assets, both physical and human. The progress of technology produces cheaper substitutes for machines and skills which have been acquired by investment. Assets specialized in the production of given commodities have the whole or part of their values destroyed if new, better, or cheaper substitute products are discovered. The owners of both physical and intangible capital are damaged by innovation.

5. Gainful, useful, and valuable activities have unwanted, harmful side

effects. Therapeutic treatment for some diseases induces others; the transport of people and goods produces accidents that damage vehicles and people; the production of some commodities generates wastes which, when disposed of, pollute air and water; if one constructs a building, he may cut off the view of green fields and running streams of another; the taking of ore and lumber to provide useful goods destroys the aesthetic quality of the environment; coal mining causes black lung, stored volatile goods explode, and oil drilling fouls beaches.

6. Some behavior activates the state's power to punish. John Doe takes the assets of Richard Roe without his consent, or assaults him, or burns his property, and the criminal justice machine begins to grind. This is the class of criminal harm-doing.

Society is prepared to accept some classes of harm because more highly valued objects are thought to be achieved by doing so. Foresight, skill, shrewdness, invention, and innovation are the qualities that generate material progress and improvement in the material conditions of life. If rewarding those who possess abundant quantities of those qualities bankrupts others or diminishes the value of their assets, it is thought to be just as well, all things considered.

While the social acceptance of harm in the playing of the business competitive game is clearly seen, a similar social attitude toward side-effect harm is not so obvious but can easily be demonstrated. These side effects are probabilistic events. They can be avoided in the sense that resources employed in particular ways will reduce the probability numbers associated with given unwanted occurrences, but society behaves as if only some harmful side effects are worth avoiding. In a certain sense, this is consistent with rational social behavior, even if the rational calculus producing the observed outcome is not usually worked out explicitly.

Consider, for example, the case of children who are transported to and from school on school buses. Almost every year some of them lose their lives because the school bus is struck by a moving train at a level railroad crossing. Every child riding a bus whose route carries it over a level railroad crossing is subject, at some probability, to the loss of his life. Some loss of life of children can be avoided by reducing the probability that the collision will occur; this can be done by relocating schools, or having buses travel longer distances to avoid the level crossing, or constructing overpasses at the tracks. But time has value and alternative uses, as do concrete, steel beams, reinforcing rods, grading equipment, and man-hours of labor. That any of these resources are put to uses other than constructing schools or overpasses or longer routes to school implies the willingness to give up the lives of children as a price for whatever utilities are produced by the use of these resources for other purposes.

Experience is rife with analogues. There would be less damage to persons and property if hills were leveled when roads are built, if roads were straightened, if road travel were done at lower speeds, if fewer roof leaks were repaired (thus fewer ladders would be climbed and fewer would fall from ladders), if high windows were washed less often, if less coal were mined, and if less metal were machined (so that less cutting oil and grease were handled).

We observe that some things are done and other things are not done and that avoidable harm is a consequence. This occurs because avoidance is costly and some incremental quantity of harm is preferred to the use of avoidance resources.

The Optimalization of Harm

Some quantity of harm greater than zero is optimal. A rational, calculating society would prefer to experience harm to the point where the last unit of harm prevented has a value just equal to the value of the resources employed in preventing that unit of harm.

This is a principle that can be applied as well to the prevention of criminal harm as to harm of other classes. Take arson. In this country in a recent year there were 7,000 arrests in which the arrested person was charged with that offense. There were, in addition, undetected cases and detected but unsolved cases. Arson puts human and real assets in peril and damages them. The quantity of arson is affected by the magnitude of the probability that arsonists are identified and punished. The quantity of damage done is affected by the number of burnings that occur with intent to damage, by the quantity and quality of fireproofing materials used in construction, by the extent of caution exercised in the use and storage of combustibles, by the number and efficiency of installed sprinkler systems and the logistical disposition of fire extinguishers, and by the quantity of public fire-fighting resources ready to respond to reports of fires.

Any given observed quantity of harm done by arsonists can be, in principle, reduced to zero. But doubtless it does not pay to go so far. The cost of preventing damage will, beyond some point, exceed the damage forestalled by prevented arson or by diminished consequences of its occurrence. How much harm from arson should a rationally calculating society be prepared to suffer? The condition for achieving the optimal quantity of harm is that already presented: the last unit of forestalled harm and the instruments and strategies employed in forestalling that unit of harm should have the same value. The failure to fulfill that condition and, thus, the occurrence of a smaller quantity of harm than that implied by the satisfaction of the condition mean that social waste is experienced, for things of greater value would then be consumed in the achievement of things of lesser value.

We operate more or less consistently with that principle. There are less fireproofing, fewer sprinkler systems, fewer extinguishers, fewer fire fighters, and fewer solved arson cases than there can be; there is, therefore, more damage from arson than there can be. It is not here asserted that refined calculations are done of marginal costs and gains, but only that some harm is considered worthwhile because it costs too much to prevent it and, therefore, that the calculation is roughly done.

Just so with respect to other classes of criminal harm. Taking crime statistics, for the moment, at their face value (of course, they should not be so taken), we have in this country, in each year, about 12,000 murders and nonnegligent manslaughters, 27,000 rapes, 202,000 robberies, 250,000 aggravated assaults, 1,600,000 burglaries, and over 650,000 auto thefts. Some of them can be prevented by employing more, and more efficient, prevention resources. But the cost of preventing all crimes in any of the enumerated classes would consume a grotesque enormity of resources; the game would not be worth the candle. So it pays to suffer some quantity of each of them.

There are a number of alternative strategies of crime prevention, and what society wants to do is to apply that strategy in the set of all strategies which will minimize the cost of achieving the optimal quantity of crime in each class.

All of the alternatives impose cost upon criminals. The costs may be a payment in kind—time spent in prison or in enforced labor—or a money payment—as a fine or compensation required to be paid to victims, or the psychic pain of the sensation of guilt, or the discomfiture of banishment or ostracism, or asset costs (tools must be acquired to force access to locked premises or time must be spent in pursuing victims who have hidden), or income forgone in some legal occupation when time is, alternatively, spent in the pursuit of a criminal career.

Some of these costs are de facto imposed only upon those who are identified as having behaved criminally, are taken into custody, are charged, and are convicted. Not all who misbehave are convicted. The expected cost confronting one who contemplates engaging in criminal behavior, therefore, is the product of the estimated value of the cost, if imposed, and the probability that the cost will be imposed. Thus, more police, quicker police response to crime reports, more efficient detection and interrogation processes, more comprehensive police files and more rapid communication of their contents, and better alarm systems all raise the cost of doing business by increasing the probability of apprehension and conviction and, therefore, increase the expected cost to the criminal.

It is important to understand, in this connection, that there is no significant difference, for our purposes, between preventing crime per se and punishing those who successfully consummate a criminal act. Locking doors, building fences, purchasing dogs, and doubling police patrols prevent crimes from being committed by making it more costly to commit them. In the same way, increasing punishments of convicted persons and increasing probabilities that malefactors will be discovered prevent crimes from being committed by making it more costly to commit them.

The magnitude of the cost to criminals of following a criminal career or perpetrating a single criminal act is a function of cost incurred by the community. High fences are socially more costly than low ones; sensitive alarm systems that are better distinguishers of criminal from noncriminal intruders are more costly than insensitive alarms; two-man patrols are more costly than one-man patrols; long prison terms are more costly in terms of prison care and forgone prisoner output than short terms; high fines and charges of more serious offenses are more costly than low fines and charges of less serious offenses because they generate stronger defenses, more testimony, and longer trials; deeply felt guilt is more costly than that only superficially felt because it requires more intensive education on the negative value of sin and more attention to forming community consensus. Because it pays society to spend only so much to prevent crime, it follows that it pays to impose only so much (not less and not more) cost upon criminals and to experience the quantity of crime that cost to the criminal will produce, given expected gains from criminal behavior.

The rational decision-making rules being expounded here require that criminal harm be costed. Crimes are, of course, whatever legislatures declare them to be. What is legal in one jurisdiction may be illegal in another.

The Hidden Benefits of Crime

Not all crimes are, however, clearly harmful. Indeed, some crimes are socially gainful. The violation of laws that inhibit productive behavior causes the community's output to rise. In general, the rule of free trade among and within nations is a resource allocation rule superior to those that constrain trade. It follows from this that smugglers, illegal overseas investors, black marketeers, unlicensed practitioners in trades and professions, and evaders of legal price and rent controls cause the average material level of life of the populace to be improved.

Consider now the case of freely engaged, consensual transactions in illegal commodities. A prostitute's or an abortionists's services are contracted, a wagering transaction is made, a child's labor is purchased (say, with the consent of his parents), money is borrowed at usurious rates. There is no compulsion either to buy or to sell. These transactions are on all fours with the purchase and sale of eggs or cars or an orthodontist's services. There is a presumption of mutual gain in the exchange. If it were not worth the while of both contracting parties, the exchange presumably would not have been consummated.

Harm does not seem to befall third parties who are outside the transaction.

The defenses for illegalizing some commodities sometimes feign harmfulness, but they are defenses that do not hold much water. If Jane Doe sells carnal services to Richard Roe, others suffer aesthetic displeasure; violence is done to their standards of right conduct even if the act is done privately, out of sight of others. But if Jane Doe buys a low-cut or backless gown or Richard Roe a flamboyant necktie, others may also be aesthetically displeased. Consider that third-party harm is done in the one case, and it is done in the others. Once on this road, the journey is endless.

Or the harmfulness claim may take another form. A bettor may lose; he ought to be protected from doing harm to himself. But if he climbs a ladder, he may fall; if he drives an auto at 40 miles per hour, he may run into a bridge abutment; if he operates a machine with moving parts, his finger may be caught; if he marries, she may quickly prove to be a shrew; if he drills for oil, he may find a dry hole. This road also is endless. The criminal law does not seem to be an appropriate instrument for forestalling harm to one's self on other grounds as well. Risk preference and risk aversion are unequally distributed in the population; utility will be maximized, therefore, if risky ventures are not forestalled but, rather, if individuals are permitted freely to distribute themselves among risky and secure ventures. Risky ventures forestalled imply gains forestalled; roofs will go on leaking if ladders are not climbed, and ore-bearing bodies will not be found if they are not searched for. And, finally, the suffering of adverse consequences when risky ventures fail is a splendid didactic instrument; if costs are to be levied upon risk-takers, there is no reason why costs imposed by the law are to be preferred to costs that are inherent in failure.

The claim that consensual transactions in illegal goods and services are harmful rests on quicksand. It is a claim without merit. Because such transactions do no damage to their parties, they are socially costless when they occur. It follows that society wastes its resources when it employs them to prevent such transactions.

Of a piece with these harmless crimes are those involving single-person behavior that affect others only in the sense that they are visually displeasing. About a third of all arrests made in the United States are for drunkenness, and a large number of arrests are made for such offenses as vagrancy and loitering. It is hard to see that any harm is done by a public drunk, and the enormous resources spent to take drunks into custody and process them through the criminal justice system seem almost pure waste. Indeed, it is worse than this. Since harmless persons are deprived of their liberty, the system produces a discommodity or a negative product.

The Costs of Crime

Consider another class of crime—the taking of another's wealth clandestinely. How is one to measure the social cost of such acts so that rational decision rules can give guidance on the assignment of the appropriate quantity of resources to prevent them? If gifts are freely given, the economics fraternity labels them "transfer payments" and considers that the wealth and income of all, taken together, has neither risen nor fallen, except possibly in one sense. If the utility of the transfer payment (including the utility of that which is given but excluding the utility of the act of giving) is larger for the receiver than for the giver, aggragate income can perhaps be thought to have risen; if it is smaller, aggregate income can be thought to have fallen. Since the utility of income falls with the rise in the quantity of income possessed by an individual, it is sometimes thought that aggregate real income will rise if transfer payments flow from rich to poor. If the possibility of making interpersonal utility comparisons is rejected, then of course the immediately foregoing judgment is estopped. Analogously, a clandestine transfer payment—as in any form of thievery, fraud, or embezzlement—will be socially costly or socially gainful, depending upon whether the mean income of thieves, defrauders, and embezzlers is less or more than the mean income of their victims.

Clandestine transfer payments are, however, clearly socially costly in other senses.

First, the theft of one's property is like a 100 percent tax on that fraction of it which is taken. The mathematically expected tax rate is 100 times the probability that theft will occur. It is possible, but not certain, that empirical magnitudes are such as to produce disincentive effects. Uncertainty of retention—that is, insecurity of possession—may cause less income to be produced. Some quantity of time that would otherwise be expended in income-generating activities is instead spent in other ways. The output of goods and services is smaller by some increment.

Second, precautions are taken to prevent theft. Safes, vaults, safe-deposit boxes, mirrors, the services of guards, the accumulation of information to defend one's self from fraud, and the services of accountants examining books to defend against embezzlement all take in their making resources that have alternative valuable uses. Society loses, by theft, whatever other things those resources would have been used for.

Third, the existence of theft produces uncertainty, since it is known only ex post which members of the population will be victimized. Uncertainty is costly.

The costing of crimes that destroy or damage assets is more forthright. Sometimes it is even unnecessary to search out proxy or shadow prices. Arson that burns a house to the ground costs the market value of the house. Vandalism that willfully and maliciously defaces property costs the difference between the property's value before and after defacement.

Temporary theft—the case of stolen property that is recovered and restored to its legal owner—is in approximately the same class. Its cost may be thought to be equal to the rental value of the property for the time during which the owner has been deprived of its possession plus some sum to compensate him for the absence of his consent to the consummation of the rental "transaction."

The costing of destruction and impairment of human assets, as by criminal homicide and assault, does require the search for proxies. How much is it worth society's while to spend in the prevention of one more murder? The amount that will be lost to society if the murder is not prevented. How much does society lose if a murder occurs? The output the prematurely deceased person would have produced if his life had been prolonged (if the murder had been prevented), perhaps net of what he would have consumed in that extended remainder of his life, discounted at some appropriate time rate (since his output in the distant future has less value, per unit, in the present than his output in the near future), plus any resources employed in medical therapy prior to his death, plus the cost of the failure to postpone burial expenses, plus the value of the grief of his kin. His income foregone by his murder is an appropriate proxy for his output and some proxy (I cannot suggest which) would have to be sought out for the monetary evaluation of grief.

The cost of impairment is computed in the same way. An assault may destroy an eye or merely cause one to be bedridden for a week. In either case output is lost. The sum of the values of that output, discounted, of medical therapy, perhaps of prosthetic appliances, and of pain is the cost of assault. A proxy for the value of pain may be constructed by the manipulation of wage differences in painful and painless occupations, or it may be constructed, for example, by observing the relative frequency with which people are unwilling to submit to painful therapy when the magnitudes of the probabilities that a disease will produce illness of given dimensions and that the illness will be terminal, if therapy is not undergone, are known.

It may seem offensive to some that murder and assault are approached so unsentimentally as is implied in their money valuation. But this is consistent with behavior in the most moral societies. First, workmen's compensation statutes specify the value put on the loss of an eye or a finger, and juries and judges by the hundreds sit every day in tort proceedings to decide the values of lives and limbs taken in accidents. Second, every community at every time employs some number of policemen, and not one more than that number, when employing one more presumably would forestall an assault by diminishing the probability of its occurrence. The failure to employ one more, therefore, implies the prior judgment that it is not worthwhile, given the cost of doing so, to forestall that assault. Implicit comparative valuation is done.

We come now to the costing of probabilistic criminally harmful behavior. It is often a crime to drive while drunk or to carry a weapon. If drunken drivers produce an accident once in every 100 times that they drive and if accidental damage averages $10,000 in value, then each act of drunken driving produces 1/100 of $10,000 in damage. If a gun is fired once in every 200 times it is carried and if on each firing it does an average of $20,000 in damage, then each act of carrying a gun does 1/200 of $20,000 in damage. For refinement, adjustments would be made. The expected damage from drunken driving will be affected by the intensity of drunkenness (measured, perhaps, by the quantity of alcohol in the blood, adjusted for the girth and height of the drunken person), the quality of the road traveled, the weather, and the density of traffic. Thus different costs can be associated with different subsets of drunken driving. The carrying of guns by some puts fear in others, and the value of this fear would be summed with other damage done by the gun's use. Valuation of fear might be measured by examining the costs people are willing to incur to keep out of harm's way.

So much for the costing of particular classes of crime.

The cost of crime, all taken together, is somewhat more complex than simply aggregating the costs of separate crimes. One can think of a society in which the propensity to commit crime is zero. By this it is meant that criminal harm would not be done even if no parent nor preacher nor teacher expended time and energy in communicating the principles of right behavior to children, or teaching them how to distinguish right from wrong behavior, or persuading them to follow righteous paths; and criminal harm would not be done even if it were known with certainty that there was no system of social apparatus for imposing costs upon criminals. In such a society the cost of crime would be zero.

If, however, the propensity to commit crime is positive, then, even if no crime is committed, it would be because society had incurred costs of crime prevention. In that case it would be appropriate to count the cost of prevention as a cost of crime because the cost of prevention comes into existence only because crimes would otherwise be done.

The cost of crime, therefore, turns out to be the sum of the cost of successfully consummated crime and the cost of preventing crime. This is true despite the fact that the magnitudes of these numbers are inversely related. The higher the cost of prevention (the larger the quantity of resources employed in prevention), the larger the number of forestalled crimes, the smaller the number of consummated crimes, and, therefore, the smaller the cost of consummated crime.

It needs to be kept in mind that police, courts, probation officers, and prison systems are not the only crime preventers. So is the whole complex of social control machines in homes, schools, and churches that teach obedience and inveigh against wrong and harmdoing. So is the set of alternative legal occupational opportunities. And so, finally, is private caution. For any given level of criminal harm to be experienced by society, an increment of improvement in any one of these can be compensated for by diminished effort by the others.

This raises an interesting question about the combination of crime control strategies. In principle, police, teachers (that is, that part of teachers' time devoted to teaching obedience or conformity), and burglar alarms should be combined in those proportions that will minimize the cost of preventing the desired number of burglaries. Cost minimization will be achieved if the condition of equimarginality is fulfilled. This means that costs will be minimized if the last, say, 100 dollars spent for each— police, teachers, and alarms—will forestall the same number of burglaries. If this condition is not fulfilled, it pays society to use less of some control strategy and more of another.

In the reckoning of optimal strategy combinations, the gains from forestalled crime must have netted out of them all costs associated with the control strategies. There are some costs associated with prevention through public criminal justice systems that are not associated with private prevention methods. The police sometimes invade privacy by eavesdropping; they sometimes employ excessive force; the courts sometimes convict and punish the innocent; prisons are sometimes institutions for teaching criminal skills and forging criminal coalitions. Locks and safes do not harm in this way.

Eavesdropping and the use of force appear to generate gains, for they would seem to cheapen the cost of information acquired by the police and, therefore, the cost of identifying criminals. We reckon them here to have negative value, not only because privacy and freedom from laceration by truncheons are desired commodities but also because the use of force and eavesdropping violates the rules of due process, which are calculated to distinguish the guilty from the innocent. It is essential that the distinction be drawn. If it is not and both guilty and innocent persons are punished indifferently, a disincentive system designed to achieve good behavior by punishing misbehavior ceases to exist. In the polar case, those to be punished would be selected at random from the whole population. If the incidence of punishment were independent of the distribution of misbehavior among individuals (that is to say, if whether one is punished or not does not depend on whether one has behaved badly or well), then the quantity of misbehavior in society can be expected to rise. Appearances, thus, turn out to be deceptive. It only seems that violation of due process will make the police more efficient, increase the probability of apprehension of criminals, raise the cost of doing criminal business, and lessen the quantity of crime done. In fact, our expectations are precisely contrary to this. Violation of due process fuzzes the distinction between criminals and noncriminals. Punishment is inappropriately distributed in the population. A wrong signaling system is constructed. The outcome is more criminal behavior, not less.

A complete model will produce a combination solution that will employ more private caution and less public sector preventive activity than would a model omitting as variables the harm that can be done by police, judges, juries, and prison guards.

The accomplishment of the optimal combination of public and private crime prevention activity does not require specific direction to private persons with respect to the quantity of caution they should appropriately take. Each can be expected to exercise that amount of care which takes account of the magnitude of losses that would be suffered if he were the victim of a crime and the estimated probability that he will be victimized.

A diminished quantity of policing, by enlarging that probability number, can be expected to increase the care taken. It suffices, therefore, for the public sector to choose the proper size of its own crime-prevention effort to secure a proper complementary quantity of private effort.

The Distribution of the Costs of Crime

Victimization probabilities vary among individuals. If official crime statistics are to be believed, women are more likely to be raped than men; nonwhite women are about four times more likely to be raped than white women; and women with incomes of less than $3,000 are 4.5 times more likely to be raped than women with incomes over $10,000. The chance that a nonwhite will be the victim of aggravated assault is twice that for whites. Robbery rates are almost 20 times as high in cities of over 1 million people as in places with populations of under 10,000.

The optimal quantity of care to take varies with, among other things, one's age, race, sex, income class, and place of domicile. The larger the net expected value of loss from victimization by crime, the larger the expenditure warranted to avoid victimization. We observe, indeed, that more sophisticated locks are installed on doors in New York City than in smaller places.

If one wanted to determine the distribution of the costs of crime among individuals, it would not suffice to examine the distribution of victimization. This is because market adjustments can make costs incident upon others. This is equivalent to saying that the true distribution of victimization and its apparent distribution diverge.

Consider, for example, shoplifting. The apparent victim is the shopkeeper. But, on the simplifying assumption that shoplifting losses are proportional to sales in all shops, shoplifting has the same effect as a uniform tax on shop sales and, as all economists know, the losses would be divided between shopkeepers and the buyers of their goods or services. The fractional division of shoplifting losses between shopkeepers and buyers depends in part upon the extent to which buyers are responsive to changes in shop prices. The less responsive they are, the larger is the share of the losses borne by them; the more responsive, the larger is the share of losses borne by shopkeepers. Relaxing the simplifying assumption does not impair the analysis. If shoplifting tends to be concentrated in ghetto shops, shopkeepers will bear a large part of the cost if ghetto shoppers have good, convenient buying alternatives outside the ghetto, and shopkeepers will bear a small part of the cost if ghetto shoppers do not have such alternatives.

Or consider the incidence of the cost of assault and the unequally distributed spatially. Real property values will be the market to take account of the difference in risk among neig Other things being equal, the price and rental value of housi _...-gerous places will be lower than they would be if these places were safer. Consumers of housing services in unsafe neighborhoods will be somewhat compensated for the risks they run by lower prices for housing of given quality or by being saved the cost of daily transport to and from the suburbs. Owners of housing in those places will have acquired their properties at lower prices—reflecting lower income and service streams they will yield over time—than they would have been required to pay if the places experienced less crime. These expectations will be altered, of course, if a change in crime rates occurs. If a neighborhood becomes relatively more crime-prone, those who own immovable real assets in it will lose some of the value of their assets; if a neighborhood becomes relatively less crime-prone, property owners in it will have capital gains.

Institutional arrangements can alter the incidence of the cost of criminal harm. Insurance will spread the cost over insured persons. Compensation paid the victims from community funds will spread the cost over taxpayers. The shifting of the cost of crime from explicit victims to others who are victimized only in a probability sense will diminish the quantity of caution taken and therefore, by diminishing the cost of doing criminal business, will increase the quantity of crime committed. In the aggregate, all have as much incentive for taking care as if only ex post victims bore criminal costs, for the forestalling of crime by care would reduce insurance premiums and taxes. But precautionary effort exerted by any member of the community spreads its benefits to all. Since insurance and victim compensation schemes externalize gains, the total quantity of precaution will be less under such arrangements.

A relevant question here is who should appropriately bear the cost of crime. This is a question to which there is no possible response until some desired objective is defined and it can be deduced how far different distributions of crime costs will tend to cause that objective to be achieved. The objective may, or may not, include an equity component. It would not do so if it were, for example, defined to be the minimization of criminal harm, subject to some expenditure constraint. It would include such a component if the objective were the same as the foregoing but with the additional constraint that harm done the elderly be held to zero.

Let us assume an equity-free harm-minimization objective. Upon reflection, it can be perceived that crime, when it occurs, is often a product of the combined behavior of criminals and victims.

Persons suffer criminal harm because they have not put themselves out of harm's way. They would not have been assaulted if they had not crossed wooded parks at night, or walked deserted streets, or lived in unguarded apartment buildings, or refrained from installing a third lock, or done the laundry in the basement, or failed to move to the suburbs.

What is wanted is an allocation of the cost of criminal harm that will produce a signaling system which will induce an amount of avoidance cost to be incurred by individuals such that only the appropriate quantity of criminal harm is done. The diffusion of the cost of harm among the populace while harm itself is, ex post, not diffused but concentrated, separates the incidence of cost from the generation of harm, in the sense that victims generate it by avoiding harm-avoidance costs. That is to say, insurance and victim-compensation schemes dampen the intensity of signals to exercise caution. They diminish, therefore, the amount of caution that should be taken if the harm-minimizing objective is to be served.

Compensation and insurance systems imply reimbursement of losses to victims of crime without regard to fault. Questions are not asked about the extent to which the victim's carelessness contributed to his victimization. Payment is made whether or not care has been taken and, since taking care is costly, these systems create incentives for escaping those costs. They bring an increment of carelessness into being. If explicit victims bear the cost of crime done to them, all have much stronger incentives to be careful.

This does not mean that the existence of insurance is necessarily inconsistent with social welfare maximization. Insurance somewhat increases the cost for most insured persons (those who will not have been victimized) and it greatly diminishes the cost for some (those who will have been victimized). The cost is spread, and spreading has a value which may exceed the cost of the increased quantum of crime that is produced because less care is taken. It may pay society to pay the price of an additional increment of crime for greater diffusion of loss from crime.

There is another sense in which costs can be shifted and, in the shifting, the total cost of crime can be reduced. If some illegal activities are made more costly for criminals, they will move to other illegal activities. Costs for criminals in any given activity can be increased by, for example, allocating more resources to the prevention of that activity, so that the probability of being detected and taken into custody rises for those who engage in it. By allocating police among classes of crime, the activities in which criminals engage can be structured; less of some illegal behavior can be secured at the expense of more of other illegal behavior. The combination to be rationally sought is that which minimizes the total social cost of crime. If criminals are engaged in a "wrong" set of activities, a redeployment of police can cause them to reallocate their activity among classes of victims. The reduction of aggregate crime costs may, therefore, contain the execution of negative transfer payments among different classes of the citizenry.

In much the same way crime can be moved among neighborhoods—out of some and into others—by police redeployment. It is possible to devise a decision rule that would make it rational to do this if crime for the whole community were diminished as a result of the redeployment. Put in other words, it would be rational to redeploy if the removal of some police from one neighborhood would increase crime rates there by less than those rates are reduced in neighborhoods to which the police are moved. It is clear, however, that such strategies advantage some but disadvantage others. They also produce shifts of crime costs within the community.

Crime costs can be expressed in physical as well as monetary terms, but they cannot then be summed. The Federal Bureau of Investigation publishes information, which it collects from local police departments, on the number of crimes known to the police and on the number of arrests. Everyone knows that these numbers cannot be taken as a correct expression of the physical quantity of crime that takes place in this country. There are many and complex reasons why the data are not really usable as a measure of the quantity of crime. There are many marginal crimes, like young men fighting; the numbers will be affected by whether the police treat them as crimes or as the expression of high spirits. Discretion pervades the system of charging arrested persons. The numbers will be affected by the rules laid down by police supervisors to govern the recording of crimes known to the police; a change in these rules will grossly inflate or deflate the numbers over time. The police often deliberately fudge the numbers to produce records that will maximize the probability of promotion from patrolman to sergeant or the probability of securing larger police appropriations from the city council. It can be seen that if the criterion for advancement is the clearance rate—the ratio of arrests to recorded criminal incidents—police are given incentives to record the easily solvable cases reported to them and to leave unrecorded the reported difficult cases.

The main reason that the published numbers do not correctly measure the physical incidence of crime, however, is that a very large proportion of all crime is not known to the police. Participants in consensual transactions in illegal commodities want to conceal their behavior. Victims of crime often will not report the fact of victimization because they estimate that the costs to them of reporting will exceed their gains.

The relative amount of crime that is unreported varies greatly among crimes. A 1965 presidential commission report says that, based on sample household surveys to discover the extent of victimization by crime, police were not notified of a third of all robberies, a third of aggravated assaults, 40 percent of burglaries, 90 percent of consumer fraud, and half of all sex offenses except rape. It seems likely that crime committed in this country greatly exceeds the quantity shown by police reports.

How seriously should it be regarded? What is the probability that a resident of New York City will be assaulted if he walks the streets of the city? The magnitude of that probability will vary with the physical appearance of the walker, the hour of the day, the mean income of the residents of the neighborhood, and, undoubtedly, with other variables as well. The objective risk probably is quite small, on the average.

That is to say, the fraction of all persons walking city streets at any given time who are assaulted is minuscule. Behavior is, however, responsive to subjective probability estimates, which may be very different from objective probabilities.

Risks of victimization by crime are almost always overestimated for some period after the occurrence of a crime, and the length of that period is a partial function of the magnitude of the loss imposed by the crime. When a Boston strangler is on the loose, imagination runs riot and disaster is imagined.

If in relatively "normal" times systematic underestimation of risk is not done, then, on the average, there is overestimation of risk and an excess of fear and caution. Perhaps half a million women in Boston and who knows how many more in other places shut themselves away, listening tensely for noises.

Avoidance behavior of this kind might well be the largest single component of the social cost of crime. Much of it is a product of fantasy that is generated by releases fed to the press by such agencies as the FBI. That institution is not ordinarily thought of as one which increases the country's crime cost, but it quite likely does so as a consequence of this aspect of its activity.

Study of the cost of crime reveals facets that are not obvious on its face and requires the removal of successive layers of cover for their observation. This paper has not uncovered all that can be said on the topic, nor has the complexity of interlocks been fully untangled; the paper opens the topic to its primitive beginnings. But perhaps it will usefully have demonstrated that crime and crime prevention are not so simple as they seem.

Part 2: Current Practice with Respect to Crime

4

The Problem of State Governments in Fighting Organized Crime

Arthur J. Sills

Introduction

In its general report, **The Challenge of Crime in a Free Society,** the President's Commission on Law Enforcement and the Administration of Justice commenced its chapter on organized crime by noting:

> Organized crime is a society that seeks to operate outside the control of the American people and their governments. It involves thousands of criminals, working within structures as complex as those of any large corporation, subject to laws more rigidly enforced than those of legitimate governments. Its actions are not impulsive but rather the result of intricate conspiracies, carried on over many years and aimed at gaining control over whole fields of activity in order to amass huge profits.[1]

While the President's Commission proceeded to be more specific about organized crime in America, it might be said that this opening paragraph reflects the ambiguous notion many people have about this serious crime problem today. The commission uses such terms as "society," "thousands of criminals," "intricate conspiracies," and "huge profits." All of this suggests something which functions with complete impunity, is immune from governmental action and control, and is beyond the comprehension of the average citizen.

Perhaps our failure to cope effectively with the problem has made organized crime seem invulnerable. Perhaps Americans identify vicariously with the mystique of the underworld. Perhaps we simply are on the wrong track and have not yet devised a workable formula.

Whatever the case may be, organized crime is a serious problem which affects most Americans, either directly or indirectly, every day. To the loan shark's victim whose arms are broken because he cannot pay a debt, the effect is very real. To the housewife who pays an extra penny on a product because of "extra service" rendered, the cause and effect may go unnoticed. Yet each is a victim of organized crime and each contributes to the financial power of a monolithic structure which preys on the American people.

The title of this paper is "The Problem of State Governments in Fighting Organized Crime." In order to give this subject some perspective, it is necessary to look more closely at the nature of organized crime, to evaluate public attitudes toward the problem, and to assess the basic tools which have been deemed necessary to proceed against members of the underworld.

What is Organized Crime?

It has, over the years, been popular to refer to organized crime as the Mafia, primarily because many law enforcement officials noted its striking similarity to the Sicilian Mafia. This reference has further been impregnated in the American mind because of the many studies which have treated organized crime as if, in fact, it were but an extension of the Sicilian-based underworld.[2] More recently, particularly since the McClellan hearings in 1963, the term Cosa Nostra has been heard with increasing frequency.

The use of both these terms has shortcomings. On the one hand, they tend to perpetuate the myth that organized crime is an import. On the other hand, they are offensive to Italian-Americans, who as a group are no more prone to criminal activity than is any other segment of our population.

But fundamentally, it is not important what organized crime is called— be it Mafia, Cosa Nostra, syndicate, organization, confederation, mob, or what have you. What is important is knowing what it is in the United States, how it operates, and what must be done. Authorities have gone to great lengths to decide on terminology to identify the group involved in organized crime, and all they really are doing is playing a game of semantics.

Similar futility is manifested in attempting to define "organized crime." Throughout its entire **Task Force Report,** the President's Commission makes no effort to offer a definition, but describes those characteristics which are supposed to set it apart from other kinds of criminal behavior.

The structure of organized crime is like that of a large corporation. Its ruling body is a commission (or board of directors), which is the ultimate authority on organizational and jurisdictional disputes. It is composed of from nine to 12 bosses (or presidents) of the nation's most powerful families (or divisions).

It is generally recognized that the core of organized crime today consists of 24 families or groups operating in large cities across the nation. The membership of each family varies from as many as 700 to as few as 20. It is noted that:

> Each family can participate in the full range of activities in which organized crime generally is known to engage. Family organization is rationally designed with an integrated set of positions geared to maximize profits. Like any large corporation, the organization functions regardless of personnel changes, and no individual—not even the leader—is indispensable. If he dies, or goes to jail, business goes on.[3]

The boss of each family has absolute authortiy. Beneath him is an underboss (or vice-president) and, on the same level but in a staff capacity, a counselor. Below the underboss are lieutenants, soldiers, and finally those outside the family membership who do actual work in each enterprise. Only family members are insulated from law enforcement by buffers, who serve the membership by corruption and enforcing silence. Those who do the actual work and are not members of the family have no insulation from law enforcement. They take bets, drive trucks, sell narcotics, work in legitimate businesses, and the like. They may even operate candy stores, cigar stands, or what is left of the "Mom and Pop" stores, and also accept numbers or policy bets.

The leaders of each organized crime family rely on a code of conduct to acquire and maintain positions of power. Among other things, the code gives the leader exploitative authoritarian power over everyone in the organization, requires underlings to be "stand-up" guys and go to prison while the bosses amass fortunes, and forbids informing to the outside world, interference in the leader's interests, and seeking protection from the police.

In addition to preserving leadership authority, the code renders it extremely difficult for law enforcement to cultivate informants and maintain them inside the organization. The boss himself has an elaborate system of internal informants to detect deviant members.

The two elements which make organized crime unique are corruption and enforcement. One or more fixed positions exist for enforcers, whose duty is to maintain organizational integrity by perpetrating violence against recalcitrant members, and corrupters, who maintain relationships with public officials and other influential persons whose assistance is necessary to achieve the organization's goals.

Notwithstanding, law enforcement has in recent years learned a great deal about the inner workings of organized crime, but much more knowledge of the structure and operations is needed for proper law enforcement. The President's Commission observed:

> More successful law enforcement measures against the organized crime families will be possible only when the entire range of formal and informal roles for each position is ascertained. Answers to crucial questions must be found: While it is known that "money-movers" are employed to insure maximum use of family capital, how does the money move from lower-echelon workers to top leaders? How is that money spread among illicit activities and into legitimate business? What are the specific methods by which public officials are corrupted? What roles do corrupted officials play? What informal roles have been devised for successful continuation of each of the illicit enterprises, such as gambling and usury? Only through answers to questions such as these will society be able to understand precisely how organized crime maintains a coherent, efficient organization with a permanency of form that survives changes in working and leadership personnel.[4]

Public Attitudes

In any event, one of the factors which tend to impede an effective effort against organized crime is that most people are not really frightened by it, mostly because they do not recognize it. Unlike other kinds of crime, it poses no visible threat to the individual's physical well-being. There is still a strong tendency to preserve visions of the Al Capone era and a failure to appreciate the organized criminal as the sophisticated, well-dressed businessman he is today. The absence of fear is most likely responsible, in large measure, for general indifference toward the problem. Who is afraid of a bookie or money lender? There have been numerous sensational exposés over the years which temporarily shocked the public, but the effect has always been short-lived. Some people even gain vicarious thrills, rather than revulsion, from such exposés. During the last two decades, we have had the Kefauver hearings (1951), the notorious Appalachin meeting (1957), and, since 1961, numerous special presidential messages on the crime problem. Much hope was expressed after the President's Commission issued its report early in 1967, but the only ones who listened were already well aware of the dangers which existed.

There are, of course, other factors which foster indifference to organized crime. Unlike the unorganized criminal, who is a predator, members of organized crime provide services to customers desiring the services. The individual voluntarily places a bet or plays a number because he may receive something more substantial in return. And, while the public may say, if asked, that other organized crime activities, such as loan-sharking and the infiltration of legitimate businesses, are immoral and should be illegal, it does not link these by-products with the underworld's largest source of revenues—illegal gambling.

Difficulties concerning public attitudes also stem from the manner in which the problem is often portrayed by the mass media. There is no sense of continuity, and reporting tends to be haphazard and sensationalized. Whenever an investigation occurs or a scandal erupts, certain reporters dig out their old files and recite ad nauseum ancient accounts of related and not-so-related organized crime activities. Most, if not all, of this information is well-known to law enforcement officials, but it is not the type upon which a successful prosecution can be based.

There is also a tendency by the public to view the problem of organized crime solely in terms of individual personalities. Because prosecutions against organizations are rare, the focus of public attention is usually on prominent organized crime members who themselves may never run afoul of the criminal law. Added to this is a certain degree of glamour associated with prominent underworld figures. Press coverage of Vito Genovese's funeral, for example, gave him status in the public eye which he never deserved. It was reported on the front page of almost every newspaper. Yet rarely is the death of a prominent noncriminal citizen found anywhere other than the obituary page.

Finally, it must be recognized that the difficulty in educating the public about the scope and nature of organized crime is compounded by the confidential nature of much of the information available to law enforcement officials. The American way is to provide due process and respect the rights of individuals guaranteed by the Constitution. That is why there is an obvious reluctance to reveal anything which cannot be proved in court, and there is a similar reluctance to reveal information essential to building a case. Where prosecutors are concerned, like any attorney, they are subject to the canon of legal ethics. They have an obligation to respect the rights of citizens and to avoid defamation or the misuse of information. Even if a conviction is obtained, there is still the chance that the conviction will be upset by a higher court because information was misused.

Thus, all of these factors considered, it is understandable that the general public has misconceptions about organized crime and is pessimistic or indifferent about its pursuit. Like an iceberg, it is only slightly visible from the surface, with its complex interrelated confederation submerged from public view; but also like an iceberg, its potential for harm threatens many people.

Role of State Governments

The primary adversary of the organized conspiracy must, of course, be government as exercised through its law enforcement mechanism. If there is to be a coordinated effort against the problem, it is essential that cooperation among the various units be increased and that the role of each be more clearly defined. The states, for example, are in the best position to develop information systems to serve the various law enforcement units concerned with organized crime. One of the reasons that organized crime has experienced an advantage over the years is the fragmented, often unrelated approach among federal, state, and local units of government.

In this regard, it is fair to say that the various states have been in a far more disadvantageous position to combat organized crime than have the federal and local governments. On the one hand, at least until very recently, organized crime has been viewed primarily as a problem for municipal police departments, especially in our large cities. In years past, organized crime did, in fact, concentrate its activities in large urban centers. On the other hand, the states have been viewed essentially as geographical entities containing municipal jurisdictions wherein organized crime exists. There has been very little tendency to look to state governments for leadership in fighting crime and, as a consequence, they have been bypassed by federal agencies, which have dealt directly, if at all, with local departments. State governments have been almost everywhere denied, by their own legislatures, the money, manpower, and legislative tools necessary to pursue an effective intrastate anti-crime program.

With respect to the exchange of information, areas of federal government have shown a reluctance to cooperate with state agencies. But there are promising developments to report in this regard. On February 11, 1969, the Executive Board of the National Association of Attorneys General and I met with President Nixon and Attorney General Mitchell. A by-product of this meeting was an expressed desire by Attorney General Mitchell to expand the line of communication between the Justice Department and state law enforcement agencies, with a view, among other things, to exchanging more information on organized crime, especially where possible state crimes are involved. Since that date, I have been privileged, in my capacity as President of the National Association of Attorneys General, to have further meetings with Attorney General Mitchell and members of his staff.

In recent years it has become apparent that the states should no longer play a secondary role in the effort against organized crime. The organized crime conspiracy extends far beyond municipal boundaries and, therefore, cannot be coped with effectively at the municipal level.

The times demand that state governments should assume the leadership in meeting this intrastate and interstate conspiracy. Each state, of course, has its own peculiar problems and its own peculiar capabilities. Nevertheless, certain generalizations can be made.

One of the important difficulties which must be overcome is the false asumption that the states have a chief law enforcement official with the power to pursue organized crime. Usually it is assumed that the state attorney general has such power. The fact is, however, that the power to prosecute criminals usually resides in local prosecutors or district attorneys. There are many variations in the relationship between attorneys general and prosecutors, ranging from complete control by the attorney general in some states to complete independence in others.[5] Only in Alaska, Delaware, and Rhode Island does the attorney general appear to have complete control of all details of prosecution.

Approximately half of the states permit the attorney general to initiate criminal proceedings on his own motion, thus giving him concurrent jurisdiction with the local prosecutors. Most other states authorize the attorney general to act only in limited circumstances; for example, upon request of the governor or by invitation of the local prosecutor. In New Jersey, only in December, 1968, was the attorney general empowered to seek indictments through a statewide grand jury. Previous thereto, in 1963 a Law Enforcement Intelligence Unit was created in the office of the attorney general; in 1965 an Intelligence Unit was formed in the Division of State Police, and the Law Enforcement Intelligence Unit was ultimately merged with it. In 1966 a State Police Organized Crime Task Force was established to implement information obtained therefrom. The cases developed in this fashion had to be turned over to local prosecutors for their action.

Regardless of the powers which repose in an attorney general, it has always been my philosophy that he has a responsibility to serve as spokesman for law enforcement throughout his state; he should be willing to meet and confer on a continual basis with officials at each level of government; he should constantly search for new concepts and programs to enhance the effectiveness of law enforcement; and he should propose and encourage the passage of vitally needed legislation and reform.

Substantive Criminal Law

With respect to legislation and reform, perhaps we might begin in an area which is not usually related directly to a discussion of the organized crime menace. Indeed, it is extremely important at this moment in history —when the demands placed on law enforcement seemingly far exceed its ability to repond effectively—for us to take a hard, objective look at the type of behavior we wish to proscribe by criminal sanctions. We should consider the obvious, albeit difficult, question raised by the President's Commission—how much of the present difficulty confronting law enforcement is derived from the traditional assignment to it of controlling behavior which, in light of contemporary mores, may not be a criminal problem?

Has the time come to reappraise the concept that passing a law cures social ailments? According to the report of the President's Commission, many laws which deal, for example, with drunkenness, narcotics, gambling, and irregular sexual behavior "have complicated the duties of the police, prosecutor and court and have hindered the attainment of a rational and just penal system."[6]

If we were to study our present approach to the areas of gambling and narcotics, we would be treating a substantial percentage of behavior now consuming the energies of law enforcement and a substantial percentage of organized crime profits.

We have often heard mentioned the possibility of legalized gambling controlled by the state. There are, of course, many arguments, pro and con, surrounding this issue. Those who oppose the concept suggest there is a moral issue, that the technical skill and the huge amount of capital needed would be beyond the capability of the state, and that there would be difficulty in policing the operations. Thus, they state, with the inability to police effectively, organized crime might still exert a strong influence. Objectors further state that if gambling were legalized, there would simply be more gambling. And if legalized gambling were to remove profits for organized crime, it would probably turn to corrupting other areas. Finally, it is argued that legalized gambling would not be practical because some states would have it and others would not, and thus certain areas would become havens for illegal operations.

On the other hand, we hear that certain benefits could accrue from legalized gambling. It is suggested that the state could realize revenues, for example, for educational programs, much as certain types of gambling are condoned for religious and charitable causes. Some people ask, if the public is going to continue to gamble, why the profits should not go to worthy causes rather than to the organized underworld. Prohibition is cited as a situation in which repeal eliminated a major source of organized crime profits and various revenues from excise taxes on alcoholic beverages were realized. In answer to the argument that the state could not provide the technical know-how to operate a legalized system of gambling, one observer has answered:

> The pros would, indeed, operate. On that day they would become honest citizens in the sense that hypocrisy has made them law-breakers until now. When that happens, with the single stroke of a pen, more people would become law-abiding citizens than Billy Sunday could have converted in several lifetimes.[7]

The President's Commission raised similar questions about our present approach to the problem of drug addiction. As it pointed out, even though addiction itself is not a crime, the involvement of the addict with the police is almost inevitable. An addict, by definition, is in almost constant need of drugs. Before drugs can be taken, they must be purchased and possessed, which acts are illegal. The commission report states, therefore:

> The addict lives in almost perpetual violation of one or several criminal laws, and this gives him a special status not shared by other criminal offenders . . . . (I)t also gives him a special exposure to police action and arrest, and, in areas where the addiction rate is high, a special place in police statistics and crime rate computations.[8]

Many authorities agree that our traditional punitive approach to drug addiction, like our punitive approach to drunkenness, has been a miserable failure. Certainly both problems continue to increase. But whether they would diminish or increase faster if treated in some other fashion is not an easy question to answer.

Here again the issue is shrouded by complex considerations on both sides. A primary concern of many people is that a more flexible approach would encourage the use and abuse of drugs. On the other hand, many medical experts believe it would bring the problem out in the open, where, like alcoholism, it might be treated as the medical problem which it is.

Regardless of one's point of view, the time has come to cease merely talking and to commence studying, in earnest and with objectivity, the pros and cons of the serious considerations which surround such problems of gambling and narcotics and their integral relationship to the problem of organized crime. We must attempt to seek a balance between what is and what is not in the public interest.

Consider for a moment the economics of usury, which is an organized crime product. It is not the successful, financially stable individual who turns to the loan shark for assistance. It is the marginal businessman who is unable to secure a loan from legitimate financing institutions. He is thus caught between two unfortunate alternatives: either go out of business or turn to a loan shark to stay in business. He may be a law-abiding, hard-working citizen, but because of the system and a desire to preserve what he has, he is forced to sell his financial soul to organized crime. Might we not ask if other recourse should not be provided, one which balances between what is, and what is not, in the public interest?

Before we proceed to legislation directed specifically at organized crime, it is important to mention programs which are necessary to enhance the general effectiveness of law enforcement.

Every state should have programs which require mandatory police training for all local police officials, and this should be supplemented with mandatory in-service training. Furthermore, greater provision should be made for advanced training of police officials at our various institutions of higher learning. If law enforcement is to meet the challenge of a highly professionalized and skilled underworld, then it is incumbent upon us to provide for the professionalization of our police officials. This may be a long-range concept of little immediate relief to the organized crime problem, but it is one nevertheless fundamental to our long-range success.

In addition to training, it is essential that every state enact mandatory crime reporting programs which require every law enforcement agency to report crime statistics to a central state agency. As of now, only California and New Jersey have programs that equal or surpass standards set by the Federal Bureau of Investigation for its uniform crime reporting system.

The states should likewise relieve the local police of time-consuming and often inadequate services which they are now expected to perform. For example, much police reporting today is handwritten. Mass computerization of crime data at the state level not only would be more efficient but also would relieve local police of time-consuming paperwork in which they are now involved. With respect to paperwork, most local agencies are responsible for keeping court disposition records on offenders, if any records are kept at all. This function likewise should be assumed by the state, in order that judges and prosecutors may have immediate access to a defendant's criminal history.

In any event, the point is that there are manifold areas where the states can assume the leadership in the implementation of programs which will improve the general effectiveness of local law enforcement. In so doing, they will be relieving pressures which now confront local police and which impede their more active investigation of all kinds of crime.

In addition to the aforementioned, numerous steps can be taken directly at the state level with respect to organized crime.

Organized Crime Measures

An important step would be the establishment of an agency, under the attorney general's direction, with the authority to supervise and coordinate the investigation and prosecution of organized crime. Not only should the attorney general have the power to prosecute on his own volition, but he should also have supervisory control over the county prosecutors in regard to organized crime.

In conjunction therewith, the states should provide for statewide or regional grand juries specifically for the purpose of investigating organized crime and activities related thereto. The principal need for state grand juries stems from the intrastate scope of organized crime activities, which requires a coordinated, comprehensive approach to the problem.

In addition, state legislatures should adopt witness immunity laws which grant immunity from prosecution to witnesses who would refuse to testify were they not faced with prison sentences for failure to do so. The various legislatures should enact tough anti-loan shark legislation. States should enter regional information compacts to share and pool information on organized crime of a regional or interstate nature. And they should enact anti-trust laws to prevent organized crime from muscling in on legitimate businesses and driving out business by monopoly, terror, and violence. With respect to anti-trust laws, Attorney General Mitchell has disclosed that the Justice Department is looking into the possibility of using such laws to drive organized crime out of legitimate businesses. He noted: "In organized crime's ownership of legitimate business, men tend to be a cheaper commodity than property."[9]

Law enforcement officers generally believe today that wiretapping and electronic eavesdropping are necessary tools in the fight against organized crime. Some believe they are a panacea for the problem. I am of the opinion that they are far from cure-alls but are, rather, just other devices which have limited, albeit important, utility.

Prior to the Supreme Court case of Katz v. United States, decided in December, 1967, many were of the conviction that wiretapping was constitutionally invalid under the Fourth Amendment, as applied to the states through the Fourteenth Amendment. The case of Berger v. New York, decided earlier in 1967, served to confirm this. In Katz, however, the Court held that legislation could be drafted constitutionally to provide court-authorized electronic surveillance. Certain standards were mentioned, some of which may call for further clarification.

There is no question that electronic surveillance constitutes a potential threat to individual privacy. There also exists a question whether the utility of electronic surveillance against crime is such as to outweigh the danger to personal liberties which it poses. Following the Katz case, Congress enacted the Omnibus Crime Control and Safe Streets Act of

1968, which is the enabling statute for the states. In light of Katz and the Omnibus Act of 1968, the states may now enact electronic surveillance legislation, and each legislature will have to strike its own balance. New Jersey has authorized wiretapping for a five-year period, and law enforcement officers will use it.

Computerization

There are two important areas where action should be taken in regard to organized crime's relationship to government itself. One stems from difficulties which arise in identifying, among those who obtain government contracts, persons or corporations which might be connected with or engaged in criminal interests. At the present time this requires the manual checking and cross-checking of reams of corporate papers, stockholder lists, and the like. If, however, the states were to feed all such data into a computer, it would be possible, instantaneously, to scan government contractors and reject contracts and services where there is probable cause to believe that a contractor is involved in organized crime. Many bidding statutes today provide that contracts shall be made with the "lowest responsible bidder." But "responsible" is generally thought of in terms of financial background, and there should be other considerations involved, such as connections with illegal interests.

Also in the realm of computerization, the states should consider information systems studies designed to computerize and centralize data from all of their law enforcement agencies. At present there may exist in one or more agencies certain data on individuals and corporations which would be valuable to the efforts of another agency. But because the information is not centralized and easily accessible, it is unavailable for utilization by other agencies.

For example, a State Division of Alcoholic Beverage Control or a Division of Motor Vehicles might possess information on an individual of interest to a State Police investigation. But since there is no computerized cross-reference pulling together the information from all of the agencies, the State Police might never be aware that useful information exists.

At present, the New Jersey Department of Law and Public Safety is conducting the first information systems study of its kind in the country. We have contracted with a consultant for the ultimate purpose of computerizing all relevant data now maintained by the various divisions in the department. This venture should have particular value with respect to the organized crime conspiracy and should be of interest to other states.

Campaign Funds

The other area relating to government has to do with laws regarding political campaign funds. It is through campaign contributions that organized crime often buys its way into the political system. The politician relies heavily on contributions to carry out an effective campaign. Generally, he is not in a position to question the source of the contribution and, if he were, he could not, as a practical matter, follow through with an investigation. Once the money is accepted, the politician feels obligated. If he is elected to office, the contributor may come to him for a seemingly innocuous favor. And it may well be that upon doing the favor, the politician has served as a link in an enterprise operated by organized crime.

We are not sure what the solution to this problem should be, but steps should be taken to nullify any actual or potential influence that organized crime may exert through contributions to political campaigns.

All of the aforementioned legislation and programs have been deemed important to an effective effort against organized crime. There are those, however, who say it is necessary to take a fundamentally different approach to the problem from that which we have customarily taken.

Define and Prohibit Organized Crime

The suggestion is that we attempt to define organized crime as we define other crimes today, such as burglary or larceny. Once defined, it could then be prohibited. Thus, prosecution could be sought against persons committing an "organized crime," not merely for crimes that are organized, such as bet taking or the sale of narcotics.

As a preliminary definition, one authority suggests:

> An organized crime is any crime committed by a person occupying, in an established division of labor, a position designed for the commission of crime, providing that such division of labor also includes at least one position for a corrupter, one position for a corruptee, and one position for an enforcer.[10]

This approach is of doubtful constitutional validity. Whether this can be resolved is a matter of conjecture. In any event, a bill has been introduced in the United States Senate by Senator John McClellan which, among other things, embodies a similar concept by providing additional penalties for a person committing a felony if such person is a "professional criminal" or "an organized crime leader."[11]

Conclusion

In the final analysis, however, it must be recognized that there is no substitute for more money and manpower when it comes to fighting crime. This is where our commitment has been most seriously deficient.

Whatever the reasons may be, law enforcement has traditionally been a rejected orphan, denied the degree of commitment extended to other governmental programs and services which people have come to expect. This is not to say that our priorities are out of order. The investments we are making in such areas as urban aid and education are essential and will have fringe benefits, particularly with respect to crime in the streets and conditions leading to violence. There should also be some "fallout" with respect to organized crime. Yet it still remains that the absence of a strong commitment to law enforcement is the basic source of state governments' problems in fighting organized crime, and the same implies to other levels of government and other kinds of crime.

One of the "wonderful things" about crime, insofar as politicians are concerned, is that all they need do is take a hard line and call for such measures as severe mandatory punishment. In doing so, they achieve all of the political benefits derived therefrom, without appropriating one nickel to implement essential programs necessary either to get at the causes of crime or to execute the law enforcement process effectively.

As Attorney General Mitchell recently observed: "We are tired—and we think the Nation is tired—of being promised grand schemes without the concurring commitment to adequately finance them."

Fundamentally, the solution to the problem is bound up in two words: "desire" and "capacity." Desire must be inherent in the makeup of the people entrusted with enforcement of the criminal laws. Capacity stems from the tools which are given to these law enforcement officers. Essentially, these tools consist of (1) an education to the problem, including causes and structures; (2) legislation with which to work; and (3) most important, the wherewithal to put the education and legislative tools to effective use.

Once monies are committed, however, one should not assume that results will accrue overnight. The absence of proper appropriations has placed us far in arrears in our pursuit of organized crime. But they are the necessary first step. Once they are provided to the extent needed, we shall be able to move forward. In short, let us stop merely talking about organized crime, and let us do something about it.

Notes

1. President's Commission on Law Enforcement and Administration of Justice, *The Challenge of Crime in a Free Society* (Washington, D.C.: U.S. Government Printing Office, 1967), p. 187.

2.   See, for example, Norman Lewis, *The Honored Society* (New York: G. P. Putnam's Sons, 1964); G. Schiavo, *The Truth About the Mafia* (El Paso: The Vigo Press, 1962); Edward J. Allen, *Merchants of Menace: The Mafia* (Springfield, Ill.: Charles C. Thomas, 1962).

3.   Task Force on Organized Crime, President's Commission on Law Enforcement and Administration of Justice, *Task Force Report: Organized Crime* (Washington, D.C.: U.S. Government Printing Office, 1967), p. 7.

4.   Ibid., p. 10.

5.   "The Office of Attorney General in Kentucky," Report of the Department of Law to the Committee on the Administration of Justice in the Commonwealth of Kentucky, *Kentucky Law Journal*, LI (1962-63), 1-S-152-S, see 91-S.

6.   See "Substantive Law Reform and the Limits of Effective Law Enforcement," President's Commission on Law Enforcement and Administration of Justice, *Task Force Report: The Courts* (Washington, D.C.: U.S. Government Printing Office, 1967), pp. 97-107.

7.   Jerry Izenberg, "At Large: The Great Sham," *The Star-Ledger* (Newark) (March 1, 1969).

8.   President's Commission on Law Enforcement and Administration of Justice, *The Challenge of Crime in a Free Society* (Washington, D.C.: U.S. Government Printing Office, 1967), p. 221.

9.   *New York Times* (March 28, 1969), p. 18.

10.   Donald Cressy, *The Theft of the Nation* (New York: Harper and Row, 1969), p. 319.

11.   S. 31, "The Organized Crime Control Act of 1969," Title VIII, introduced January 15, 1969.

5   The Role of the Federal Government in Combating Violence

Joseph S. Clark

Introduction

The control of violence in America has historically been considered a local problem, with major reliance placed on local police and the district attorneys. It has been apparent, however, for at least two generations that there are certain areas connected with the control of organized crime or violence—and sometimes the two do not overlap—in which local law enforcement agencies are incapable of preserving law and order while administering justice in certain wide areas of crime control. The causes for this condition are not difficult to discover.

In the first place, we have a constantly shrinking and ever more complicated world confronting us, which makes the detection and prevention of crime and violence far more difficult than it was in the 19th century.

In the second place, crime has become organized today in a way which was not the case in the halcyon days around the turn of the century— particularly in slum-ridden cities and their surrounding metropolitan areas. The drug traffic and interstate gambling syndicates are good examples.

In the third place, there are violent elements in the community which one must face up to. There are, in truth, minority groups who have a special predilection for crimes of violence, often completely personal and unorganized.

In the fourth place, local police forces and, all too frequently, the local district attorneys are not of an intellectual or moral caliber which enables them to meet the challenge presented by organized crime.

Thus, it is well established that the recruitment of competent police officers is close to being an impossibility in many jurisdictions in the United States. To reiterate a slang cliché, "Who wants to be a cop?" A policeman's life, as Gilbert and Sullivan put it, is indeed not a happy one. The threat of personal assault is always present, the pay is poor, and political considerations in many jurisdictions interfere with the selection of an adequate police force. In a tight labor market, there are plenty of well-paying jobs more attractive than the police force.

Similarily, district attorneys are all too apt to be part of a corrupt political machine, particularly in big cities, and while this is perhaps a declining phenomenon, it is not unkown that in wide areas the whole district attorney's staff is subservient to the Mafia or other groups of organized gamblers and criminals.

Finally, youth is in revolt against established authority to an extent hitherto unknown. Not long ago, students at Cornell University openly carried guns as they left a college building which they had taken over.

It is now over 100 years since Abraham Lincoln became our first President to be murdered by gun. Not very much later, James Garfield and William McKinley met the same fate.

But it was 60 years after McKinley's death before another rash of assassinations struck the country, although Franklin Roosevelt and Mayor Cermak of Chicago were both shot at while sitting on the same platform, and Cermak was killed, shortly before Roosevelt's inauguration in 1933.

More recently we have had the assassinations of John F. Kennedy, Robert F. Kennedy, and Martin Luther King, Jr., all by gun, thus bringing clearly to the forefront of public discussion the need to achieve some sort of gun control legislation.

However, before gun control became the subject of violent debate in the press, in the media, and in the Congress, with the ultimate objective of obtaining adequate Federal legislation, there was many an area in which the federal government had to step in because local law enforcement agencies had proved themselves incapable of maintaining a decent minimum of law and order, with justice and without violence. Let us take a quick survey of these areas before moving into a case study of the need for gun control legislation.

Federal Law Enforcement

There are in existence today a number of specialized federal police forces which, on the whole, do a considerably better job than their opposite numbers in local government. Perhaps this is because of superior recruiting abilities on the part of the federal bureaucracy. Perhaps it is because of better direction. Usually the pay and fringe benefits are better. A fourth reason might well be that since these federal police forces operate in a very specialized field, they are not subject to a number of the hazards and dangers which confront the cop on the boat. And finally, they have more status in the community.

Among these special federal police forces, obviously the FBI is the best-known. There is, in addition, the Coast Guard, established primarily to protect coastal shipping but also to prevent smuggling. There is the Secret Service, which protects the President of the United States and other high governmental officials and performs various other functions of a less specialized nature. There is the Internal Revenue Service, which tracks down tax evasion. There are the postal inspectors, working to prevent fraud through the mails. There is the Customs Inspection Service. There is the Treasury's Narcotics Bureau. There is the Anti-Trust Division of the Department of Justice, and its Civil Rights Division.

It may well be suggested that these are not really federal police forces and, in a generalized sense, this is true. They are, however, federal law enforcement agencies which arrest people and send them to jail. The maintenance of law and order and justice has been taken over by them in certain areas which, taken together, cover a reasonably wide spectrum of total law enforcement.

The Mann Anti-White Slave Traffic Act, passed in 1910, in many ways put the FBI into business. The Mann Act arose from a number of sensational disclosures indicating that the white slave traffic was active in transporting prostitutes across state lines and, indeed, across national boundaries. There was a great hue and cry in the Congress. The men and women of America were aroused at the threat to their daughters. In any event, the law was passed. Its enforcement was frequently abused. Blackmail was sometimes the order of the day; but eventually the procedural rule was established that the act would be enforced only where there was some commercial object in the transportation of women across state or national boundaries for immoral purposes.

On the whole, one would have to agree that the enforcement of the Mann Act has been pretty good since the early abuses were ironed out.

The next effort of the federal government to prevent crime and violence was the Dyer Act of 1919, or the National Motor Vehicle Theft Act, which dealt with the interstate theft of automobiles. Again, in the early days there was a good deal of abuse, since the act was used against juvenile joyriders crossing state lines. There was a very high level of convictions but, in many instances, the interstate gangs who were operating, for profit, the theft of automobiles across states lines as part of organized crime were pretty well ignored. However, it seems today that this useful piece of legislation has enabled a good deal of cooperation to exist between local law enforcement agents, including police, and the federal government in connection with substantially curtailing the theft of automobiles moving in interstate commerce.

The classic example of the failure of a federal law enforcement effort was, of course, the effort to enforce the Eighteenth Amendment and the Volstead Act during the era of Prohibition. Here, again, in the end the law enforcement was left largely to the federal government by many of the states. It was widely believed that the local police were either disinterested or corrupt in connection with preventing the manufacture, transportation, and sale of intoxicating beverages. Some states had their own State Police and law enforcement agents working on the business of liquor violation. Generally speaking, however, this particular branch of federal law enforcement, which of course included dealing with rumrunners, organized criminals, and bootleggers both on a commercial basis and on a smaller local basis, turned out to be such a failure that in 1933 the amendment was repealed and the Volstead Act became ineffective.

In 1930, the Division of Criminal Identification and Information was established within the FBI. This provided a national library, if you will, of fingerprints and identification which has been of great advantage to local law enforcement agents in pursuit of criminals, whether organized or not. There can be little doubt that, in this area, the FBI has done an excellent job of giving aid to local law enforcement agents in preventing violence and crime, whether organized or not.

In 1932 came the Lindbergh Law, providing strict penalties for anyone connected with an interstate kidnapping. Again, the law resulted from a particular situation. Colonel Charles Lindbergh, a national hero as a result of his solo flight across the Atlantic in a very small airplane, had his infant child kidnapped in such a way that it became very difficult indeed to identify the criminals and to punish them.

As a result, there was an enormous amount of popular uproar, and federal legislation was enacted which, in my opinion, has done some good in dealing with the problem of interstate kidnapping, a problem which is not particularly great in volume but has resulted in many a serious crime —crimes against which, in my judgment, the federal government was well justified in providing penalties.

The federal government moved again into the crime field when Franklin Roosevelt's great protégé and supporter Louis Howe persuaded him to take the lead in having a number of federal laws passed dealing with various aspects of crime. Perhaps the most notable was the Firearms Act of the early 1930's, which provided for the registration of machine guns, sawed-off shotguns, bazookas, and the like. There were, however, several other federal laws which were more procedural than substantive in nature. They did indicate, however, that the federal government was taking a continuing interest in various aspects of law and order and justice in areas where the local police and, indeed, the State Police were relatively ineffective.

But there was no federal legislation or, indeed, much interest in federal activity in the crime field between 1935, when Louis Howe's health broke down, and the advent of Robert F. Kennedy to the office of the Attorney General in 1961.

There was perhaps an exception to this which should be noted. This was the various Espionage Acts, Smith-Connolly and the like, resulting in large part from the activities of Senator Joseph McCarthy of Wisconsin, the Communist scare, and the general feeling that the federal government should enter the investigation and prosecution of treason and espionage. These acts have been of limited effectiveness, although their attempted enforcement has received great publicity. To some extent they have been ruled unconstitutional by the Supreme Court. Nevertheless, there still is federal legislation dealing with the serious crimes of sedition, treason, and the like, areas into which the state governments and local governments have been reluctant to move. (An exception was the Steve Nelson case, originating in Pennsylvania.)

As a result of an investigation conducted by a committee headed by Senator John McClellan of Arkansas, of which committee Robert Kennedy was counsel before his brother was elected President, there was a series of federal bills introduced and passed which dealt with the interstate organization of gambling. These acts have been used effectively to curtail, if not to prevent, the operations of the Mafia and other organized criminal syndicates in areas of gambling where huge fortunes were being made. Prosecution by the FBI, the Internal Revenue Service, and the federal attorney has been conspicuously more successful than that of local and state police and county attorneys. (Western Pennsylvania is a conspicuous example of successful cooperation between these federal agencies, particularly during the term of Gus Diamond, Federal Attorney from 1962 to 1969). For many years the National Police Academy has been operated by the FBI to train a limited number of local police officials in modern methods of law enforcement. This academy has deliberately been kept quite small by J. Edgar Hoover, and while it has had a limited effectiveness, it has never reached the stature anticipated by many who believed that the FBI could improve the caliber of local law enforcment.

Then came the entrance of federal marshals, the FBI, and indeed the National Guard, called out by state governors or by the federal government to deal with civil rights problems, including the unwillingness of local law enforcement agents properly to enforce the civil rights of minority groups, primarily Negroes in the South.

Again, local law enforcement broke down under the pressure of some popular sentiment among law enforcement officials, and possibly the general public, who were reluctant indeed to see the Negro obtain the civil rights to which the Supreme Court and the various Civil Rights Acts of the 1950's and 1960's entitled him.

Note must be made in passing of the enormous Congressional outcry, to some extent supported by the general public, against the decisions of the Supreme Court, such as the Miranda case and others. These cases, it was said, made it impossible to convict ordinary criminals because their civil liberties were so expanded by the courts as to make confessions no longer a very effective method of bringing criminals to justice. Moreover, the Supreme Court ruled that men charged with crimes were entitled to lawyers as soon as they were picked up. These decisions did, no doubt, prevent the conviction of some criminals. At the same time, they prevented local law enforcement officials, through brutality, fear, and the like, from obtaining admissions of guilt from individuals who, in all likelihood, were entirely innocent of the particular crime with which they were charged. There has always been a conflict between civil liberties and stringent law enforcement.

Then came the Omnibus Crime Control and Safe Streets Act of 1968, the latest intervention of the federal government into the area of law enforcement and the prevention of violence. It is no part of this paper to analyze this act, a pallid version of the legislation requested by President Johnson. It is noted here only to indicate the continuing interest of the federal government in preventing crimes of violence and also in encouraging methods of crime detection, such as wiretapping, and better methods of training of local police which are exemplified in the Act of 1968. And for the first time a President of the United States advocated a federal gun control law.

The Demand for Federal Gun Control Legislation

The following sections will be devoted to a case study of gun control legislation. It will consider how the agitation for federal gun control legislation arose, the arguments supporting such legislation and those opposing it, the impact outside events such as assassination had on arousing public opinion, the massive counterattack mounted by the National Rifle Association and its associates, publishers, and others, advancing the interests of hunters, and, finally, will consider why, as of this date, gun control legislation of any real impact has not been enacted.

In short, this will be an analysis of the workings of the democratic process in the United States at the national level, where events would seem to require legislation but the Congress, and to some extent Presidents, have been reluctant to move forward with the necessary enactments.

First, some brief background. That America has long been the most lawless of the world's nations and that statistical experts foretell a continuing increase in lawlessness was pointed out in 1960 by William H. Parker, Chief of the Los Angeles Police Department. The rate of increase in crimes of violence by gun has since then been steeper than even the most pessimistic experts had predicted.

As Richard Harris, in his analytical article in **The New Yorker** in April, 1968, pointed out:

> To foreign observers, nothing is more astonishing than our casual recourse to violence in personal disputes, unless it is our failure to restrain it by law —in particular, our failure to control the indiscriminate sale and use of guns which in recent years has lain at the heart of the controversy and at the same time has made it politically insoluble.[1]

Or, as Arthur Schlesinger, Jr., commented in his book **Violence: America in the Sixties:** "What kind of people are we, we Americans? The most frightening people on this planet." And again: "Only the Americans in the decade of the Sixties have emulated the Russians, Germans, and Japanese of the Thirties and made murder a major instrument of domestic politics."[2]

While we Americans have always been trigger-happy—perhaps an inheritance from the frontier, the vigilantes, the cowboys-and-Indians era, the conquest of the wilderness—neverthless the tendency has gotten out of hand only relatively recently.

In the 1930's, when 12 to 15 million Americans were out of work through no fault of their own, they did not go around killing either businessmen or politicians to vent their spleen.

Then came World War II and the mobilization of some 13 million Americans for the express purpose of killing enemies of the United States. They succeeded in killing well over a million of them. They were demobilized in 1945, but it was some time before the wave of violence from which we are presently suffering hit the country. In fact, despite a slowly but surely increasing crime rate, to a large extent caused by increasing numbers of crimes of violence with guns, neither President Truman, President Eisenhower, nor President Kennedy, nor, indeed, any of the major leaders of the United States Congress, with the exception of Senator Thomas Dodd of Connecticut, thought that crimes by guns were sufficiently serious a menace to the country to press for strong legislation at the federal level. It was felt that the local police and law enforcement officers, with some help from the states, could handle the problem.

It was the assassination of President John F. Kennedy with a rifle in November, 1963, which aroused the country for the first time to the menace of murder by gun. In March, 1964, a small group of United States Senators, led by Senator Dodd and by Senator Joseph Tydings of Maryland, and an even smaller band of Congressmen, attempted to persuade the Judiciary Committees of the two branches of Congress that federal gun control legislation should be cleared for floor action. Local enforcement, they felt, was inadequate.

President Johnson, a Texan reared in the gun-toting tradition of the West, hung back. Then in April, 1968, Martin Luther King, Jr., Nobel Peace Prize winner and the hero of many a liberal, white as well as black, was gunned down in Memphis, Tennessee, by an assassin with a rifle.

Finally, in the early summer of 1968 Senator Robert F. Kennedy, formerly Attorney General of the United States and the brother of the martyred President, was killed by a pistol shot by a madman in Los Angeles after he completed a speech on the night of the California Democratic primary. One would think that these three spectacular assassinations would have moved the Congress and the President to action. The Congress did indeed take some steps forward, but the President hung back until the late fall of 1968, when he finally came out for immediate action, but he was too late to be of much use to the proponents of strong gun control legislation.

. A tame and pallid section dealing with gun control emerged from the Safe Streets and Crime Bill of 1968, a most unsatisfactory piece of legislation in many regards but one which President Johnson finally decided to sign because, he said, it had more good than bad in it.

All the law did was to prohibit the sale in interstate commerce of short guns, i.e., pistols and revolvers, or the purchase of these weapons outside the home state of the purchaser. There are no provisions for registration or for licensing. Although the Senate had passed a bill which would have dealt with long guns or rifles in the same way, as the House did, this was stricken out in conference and does not appear in the final legislation. The act also prohibits the transportation or possession of pistols by persons under indictment, fugitives, felons, adjudged mental incompetents, and those dishonorably discharged from the army, but provides no means to prevent such persons from making firearms purchases.

Senator Tydings and his colleagues are again at the business of attempting to persuade the Congress that a decent federal gun control act is essential to minimize the number of deaths by gun in the United States. There is a new President in the White House and he, as did his predecessors for many years, hangs back and seems to believe that the remedy is stronger penalties for those who commit crimes with guns rather than preventive measures which might reduce the death toll.

The purpose of Senator Tydings' bill, which is supported by an overwhelming majority of the American people, is to assure by federal legislation, if the states refuse to act, that no guns are purchased or possessed by criminals and other categories mentioned above, and to make this provision enforceable by requiring the registration and licensing of all firearms in order to help the law enforcement activities of district attorneys and police, so that when gun crimes are committed, arrest and conviction of the offender will be expedited. The entire point of this bill is to enable the police to keep a registry of serial numbers and other identifying marks of guns in private possession to enable them to solve crimes and to deny access to firearms to very special categories of dangerous people. It should be stressed that nobody, least of all Senator Tydings and his colleagues, has ever suggested that any law-abiding person should be denied ownership of a gun. A citizens would be as free to hunt or to shoot, after the law is passed, as he is today.

Pros and Cons of Federal Gun Control Legislation

Let us now take a look at some of the basic facts which are relevant to the argument between those who propose and those who oppose strong gun control legislation.

The FBI reports that there were 130,000 gun crimes committed last year, and the number appears to be growing. Since 1965, for example, the gun murder rate is up 47 percent, aggravated assault by gun is up 76 percent, and armed robbery committed with guns is up 58 percent. There were 7,600 gun murders in the United States last year. Let me give you a couple of examples of what I am talking about.

In New York's Central Park not too long ago a man barged into a women's lavatory, killed a young girl whom he had never met, then climbed to the roof to fight it out with the police who swarmed in on him. He wounded two policemen and killed an old man, who happened to be nearby, just for fun—the old man had nothing whatever to do with the crime which was being perpetrated.

Here's another: The robber of a sandwich shop in Baltimore, Maryland, made four people lie facedown in a row on the floor. None of them had resisted him. He shot each in turn and then went back and shot them all again.

These are the kinds of senseless murders committed, in all likelihood, by people who are deranged. They are going on every week in all the big cities of our country. It is important to notice that very few crimes with guns are committed by legitimate hunters. The problem is not with hunters. The problem is with the efforts of some of the hunters to prevent the law enforcement agencies in the country, largely in the cities, from tracking down and catching and convicting criminals who are engaged in murder, aggravated assault, and armed robbery with guns.

Indeed, it might be said that the controversy is largely one between the cities, which need protection against murder, and the rural areas, which do not seem to understand the need for the kind of legislation being sought.

A good example is the recent University of Chicago study of homicides in that city, which showed that the death rate is about five times greater in gun attacks than it is in other forms of violent crimes; and that these homicides often result from attacks which are not at all motivated by a desire to kill. Therefore, the deadliness of the weapon becomes the key determinant of the homicide rate. This Chicago study concluded that the absence of firearms would depress the otherwise expectable homicide rate.

In Philadelphia, where I used to be the mayor, the police, and notably Frank Rizzo, the present Chief of Police, feel that Philadelphia's model City Gun Ordinance has been an extraordinarily good deterrent to crimes committed with guns. Philadelphia has the lowest murder rate of any of the 10 largest cities in the country. Rizzo attributes this, to a significant extent, to the gun ordinance. Unfortunately, however, the ordinance can have no extraterritorial effect, and anybody can bring a gun in from a surrounding state without registering it or getting a license. So we can do very little about gun identification or prevention of gun crimes in the city, unless the criminal happens to be a resident of Philadelphia who has obeyed the ordinance and has registered and licensed his gun. In that case, if he is found with an unlicensed and unregistered gun and is, in fact, a criminal with a prison record, he will be sent to jail for illegal possession.

Needless to say, the district attorneys and the police chiefs of the country have gone on record as indicating the need for legislation which would require the registration and licensing of firearms.

Attorney General Sills of New Jersey has cited the provisions of the effective New Jersey Gun Control Act and pointed out the enforcement difficulties for that state, which are quite similar to those of the city of Philadelphia because of the prospensity of criminals to cross state lines, buy guns from a jurisdiction which has no gun control legislation, and then come back into New Jersey for the purpose of shooting it out with their enemies. Nevertheless, under the New Jersey law, which requires the registration and licensing of guns, in a two-year period gun permits were denied more than 1,600 convicted criminals who would otherwise have acquired these lethal weapons. The fact that such legislation does not disturb hunters in the exercise of their normal privileges is evidenced by the number of hunting licenses granted, which increased substantially in New Jersey during this two-year period.

Nothing could be further from the truth than to suggest that adequate gun legislation does not seriously reduce crime and work very much to the advantage of law and order all over the country. This, I believe, is established beyond dispute by the basic facts and all the experience that we have had to date.

It is equally apparent that a large majority of the American people desire the protection which strong gun legislation could give them and their fellow citizens, particularly in urban areas. The Gallup Poll has shown that popular support for gun legislation and licensing runs around two-thirds of all the people surveyed. The Harris Poll is even higher. It shows 73 percent of the people in favor of such legislation. My own mail, while I was a member of the Senate last year, when the gun control legislation was at its most controversial, ran initially about 12 to 1 in favor of strong gun control legislation, including licensing and registration. This was during the period between the murder of Martin Luther King, Jr., and the murder, several months later, of Robert F. Kennedy. The National Rifle Association, however, mounted a massive campaign of a lobbying nature to try to persuade the Senators and Congressmen that their mail was deceiving them and that a majority of the American people really were opposed to this legislation. Even after this effort had been running along for a good many months, my mail still ran from 2 to 3 to 4 to 1 in favor of registration and licensing.

The difficulty with all these popular tests of opinion is that those who passionately oppose a given measure, whether it be civil rights, or peace in Vietnam, or gun legislation, are the very ones who make the biggest noise and are what might be called one-issue citizens. They care nothing about adequate measures to protect our minority groups, to feed the hungry, to stop the killing of American boys in the jungles of Asia, to take care of the poor, or to improve our educational system. The only thing they are really interested in is prevention of enactment of legislation which would contribute to law and order and cut down crime in the streets, because they are under the mistaken belief that such legislation would, in some undescribed way, limit their possession and use for hunting purposes of the weapons they now own. The irrationality of their views is almost psychotic.

As Senator Tydings of Maryland puts it:

> The Gun Lobby, like any other extremist single-issue organization, has been able to make its voice heard louder and longer than any other group. Supporters of reasonable gun control tend to be multi-issue people willing to judge their representatives on a variety of issues. But the gun extremists make their judgment on the gun issue alone. And single-issue people frighten officeholders more than any other threat.[3]

Here are a few of the more pertinent facts brought to light by Senator Tydings and his colleagues:

1. Every American is 35 times more likely to be murdered by gun than is a Briton, a Dane, a German, or a Swede. And he is many more times likely to be killed by a gun than is a Canadian or an Australian, both from pioneer countries whose citizens conquered their wilderness and killed off the natives just as we did.

2. Since 1900, 800,000 Americans have been killed by guns. This is more than have been killed in battle in all of our wars from the American Revolution to the continuing daily deaths by battle in Vietnam.

3. Every day 21 Americans will be murdered by gun, 150 will be assaulted by gun, and 200 will be robbed by gun if the present rate of crime continues.

Let us review briefly the arguments against federal gun control. First, it is alleged that gun control legislation is unconstitutional because the Constitution provides that the right of the people to keep and bear arms shall be inviolate. This statement is indeed a naïve interpretation of the Constitution. It ignores the basic fact that the Constitution refers to the right to keep and bear arms only in connection with an organized militia. The position of the opponents of gun control has been repudiated by every attorney general who has ever held office, and by the Supreme Court as well, in the case of Miller vs. United States. Yet it is reiterated time after time by the National Rifle Association lobbyists and other opponents of gun control, who do not seem to have much regard for the truth so far as their pet issue is concerned.

Then the argument is advanced that criminals won't register their guns, and therefore a licensing and registration provision will be ineffective in preventing crime. But the proposed law would provide that if criminals don't register guns and do get caught, they go to jail for illegal possession of a gun, whether or not they have in the meantime committed another crime.

A third argument is to suggest that guns don't commit crimes, people do. But it is obviously a whole lot easier to commit a crime with a gun than without a gun, as the statistics of violence by gun demonstrate. It might be said parenthetically that automobiles don't commit crimes either. Yet nobody objects to registering his automobile and obtaining a license to drive.

A fourth argument is that the laws are adequate, they just need more enforcement. There are, in fact, some 40,000 laws dealing with the possession and use of guns on the books of various jurisdictions. But these laws, with few exceptions, are quite ineffective to assist law enforcement agencies in tracking down and indicting criminals. They don't deal with the heart of the matter, which is to require licensing and registration in order to determine what gun was used for what crime and by whom.

A final argument made by the opponents of strict gun control legislation is heard more frequently in the men's toilet than anywhere else. It is that it is part of masculinity to own a gun without any regulation whatever. As Franklin Orth, the Executive Vice-President of the National Rifle Association, told a Senate subcommittee last year, there is a very special relationship between a man and his gun. This deep relationship has its roots in prehistory, when the primitive man's personal weapon, so often his only effective defense and food provider, was nearly as precious to him as one of his own limbs. The argument has been more succinctly put by Arthur Schlesinger, Jr., in his **Violence: America in the Sixties,** as follows: "The hysteria expressed by some at the thought that guns should be licensed only strengthens the psychiatric suspicion that men doubtful of their own virility cling to the gun as a symbolic phallus."[4]

Or, as Homer Cummings, the Attorney General of the United States during the Roosevelt administration, put it: "Show me a man who is not willing to have his gun registered or licensed and I will show you a man who should not be permitted to own a gun."

The arguments made by the opponents of federal gun legislation were well summarized by Senator Tydings as follows:

> The radical right's philosophy, fears and militant racism pervade the Gun Lobby. Those who believe that foreign influences are already taking over in America naturally believe they must have guns to protect themselves. Those who hate or fear blacks and who worry about reports of armed Negro groups naturally believe they must keep guns for protection. This thinly veiled racism, common in the extremist publications of the Gun Lobby and recurrent in Congressional mail opposing gun laws, is no doubt in part responsible for the domestic arms race in our cities.[5]

And it is a domestic arms race between criminals and the police—but only because the gun lobby has killed adequate legislation.

Why There Is No Adequate Federal Gun Control Legislation

Despite the apparently ironclad case in support of federal gun legislation, and despite the indications from the Harris and Gallup Polls that the American people desire some federal assistance in stopping murder by gun, all efforts to achieve adequate gun legislation have, to date, failed. It becomes important to consider why. After each spectacular murder —President Kennedy, Martin Luther King, Jr., and Senator Robert F. Kennedy—an apparently irresistible movement arose at the grass roots to pass strong federal gun legislation. Nevertheless, each effort failed. First, the problem was getting the bills out of the Judiciary Committee of the Senate, controlled by right-wing conservatives and so-called sportsmen, i.e., hunters. Next, the House of Representatives, responding to local lobbies in many rural districts, seemed quite uninterested in any strong bill. Third, for many years the President did not support gun legislation and, when he did, he came out too late for his support to be effective.

But those of us who have studied the matter carefully believe that the principal reason that gun legislation failed after so many gun murders was that the lobby, quite amoral in its distortions of the arguments in support of gun legislation but extremely strong as a one-issue minority group in many Congressional districts (and, indeed, in many of the Western and Southern states), managed to generate a grass roots political vendetta that far outlasted the spontaneous expression of public concern. It managed its well-finished effort in a professionally effective campaign of misrepresentation and callous disregard of the public interest. Those opposing registration and licensing of guns were led by the National Rifle Association, but as a well-documented article in **The New Yorker** magazine on April 14, 1968, amply demonstrates, the NRA had many an ally among hunting groups and magazines which cater to their particular interests. Senators from states such as Idaho and Vermont, which do not have the problem of mass murder by gun and where minority groups are small in numbers, were intimidated by the gun lobby. So were most rural Congressmen.

In the industrial urban states of Pennsylvania there are more than 900,000 licensed hunters. This swing group was united by the NRA and its allies in an all-out effort to defeat candidates who supported gun registration. I personally was the victim of this attack last November. Their campaign was most effective. The next man marked for destruction by the gun lobby is Senator Joseph Tydings of Maryland, who is up for reelection in 1970. It will indeed be interesting to see whether the gun lobby, headed by the NRA, will be able to defeat him at the polls. There is no doubt they will try.

As noted earlier, politicans fear one-issue groups. And the gun lobby is certainly determined to defeat everybody in public office who wants to take effective steps to stop mass murder. In much the same way Prohibition was inflicted on the country by the Anti-Saloon League.

It is interesting to speculate on why so virulent an attack can be successfully mounted against so obvious a remedy for a clear national evil. Senator Tydings believes that the motivation is both stupid and selfish. I cannot fail to agree, since there is so little danger to any of the legitimate desires of hunters to use as many guns as they want for target practice, to kill small and large game, and for any other lawful purpose that one cannot understand the basis of the opposition in any rational way.

Nevertheless, American history affords many an instance of similar destructive efforts against clearly needed reform. The present dominance of the military-industrial complex in our life is perhaps the most striking one at the present time. We must also remember that for nearly 100 years the 13th, 14th, and 15th Amendments, assuring civil rights to Negroes and other minority groups, were defied by the Southern right-wingers, who were quite unwilling to assure the Negro the rights those amendments gave him. The effectiveness of the oil lobby in preventing any reduction in the oil depletion allowance and, indeed, in the quotas which prevent Middle Eastern oil from coming into the United States are another example. So, too, are the thus far ineffective efforts at tax reform.

I suggest that in each of these and many other cases a strongly organized and dedicated minority can hold off for a long while, if not forever, the achievement of justice through legislation supported by the President and passed by the Congress of the United States. This is one of the unfortunate results of the way democracy works in practice, as opposed to the way it is supposed to work in theory, which cause many to express grave concern with our democratic process. If, in a constantly changing and ever-shrinking world, badly needed reforms supported by a majority of the American people are to be defeated time after time by a small but stubborn minority, one must have grave doubts as to the effectiveness of our present form of government.

Conclusion

Finally, one might speculate briefly on the prospects for gun legislation which will have an impact on mass murder in our urban society. Pragmatically, I would suspect that there is not much present prospect of obtaining legislation which will carry out badly needed reform.

In the first place, President Nixon has not put the weight of his office behind strong gun legislation. In the second place, in the Senate of the United States, with two votes for each state without regard to population, there are many small states, farm states, Western and Southern states where there is no serious problem of mass murder by gun because they have a homogeneous population and relatively few large cities where citizens tend to resort to violence. Then, as in some parts of the South, there are areas where the right-wing whites are more anxious to maintain their own weapons for protection against minority groups than they are to assure that these very same minority groups are required to license and register the weapons with which they, in turn, frequently perpetrate gun murder.

Finally, the efforts of the gun lobby may be assumed to be persistent, continuous, able, and effective. Again, to reiterate the obvious, such a lobby is indeed difficult to overcome in terms of passing legislation it opposes.

It will probably take another rash of assassinations of prominent individuals or riots by students and racial minorities in which gunfire accounts for many a death to stir the Congress and the President, and indeed the country, to a state of mind in which those who are not prepared to vote for strong gun legislation will be defeated at the polls the next time they run.

To me it seems highly unlikely that this aroused public opinion can be engendered in the foreseeable future.

I conclude, accordingly, on a pessimistic note. Mass murder in America will continue for the foreseeable future and will be ended when, and only when, the President and Congress, acting as a determined unit and strongly supported by public opinion, insist on the passage of strong gun control legislation.

In other words, the federal government is not yet ready to step in to take over the responsibility which local and state law enforcement agencies carry out. Whether it ever will be is subject to a great deal of doubt.

Notes

1.   Richard Harris, "Annals of Legislation — If You Love Your Gun," *The New Yorker* (April 28, 1968).
2.   Arthur Schlesinger, Jr., *Violence: America in the Sixties* (New York: Signet, 1968).
3.   Joseph Tydings, "Americans and the Gun," *Playboy* (March, 1969).
4.   Schlesinger, op. cit.
5.   Tydings, op. cit.

6   The Supreme Court's Changing Views of Criminal Defendants' Rights

David Fellman

Background

That American public law is strongly weighted in favor of persons accused of crime is by no means a product of recent decisions of the U.S. Supreme Court. Such seminal legal principles as the rules which hold that the accused is presumptively innocent, that the burden of proving guilt rests upon the prosecution, and that guilt must be established beyond a reasonable doubt (the largest quantum of proof known to the law), have their roots in common law of considerable antiquity.[1] The solicitude of American public law for the rights of one who is accused of crime is reflected in the fact that more provisions of the federal Bill of Rights, which was ratified in 1791, are devoted to this subject than to all others, and this is equally descriptive of state bills of rights. For some centuries a characteristic feature of Anglo-American criminal justice has been, as Justice Frankfurter once observed, that it "is the accusatorial as opposed to the inquisitorial system."[2]

This tenderness of our law with respect to the rights of the accused derives from ideas distilled from long experience. It is recognized, first of all, that the abuse of police power is an inevitable mark of an unjust, dictatorial state. Modern man is apt to be quite fully aware of the terrors of an unrestrained, ubiquitous, all-powerful police force. He has reason to fear the midnight knock on the door, the resort to will-breaking interrogations, the ransacking of private dwellings without legal warrant, incarceration in barbarous concentration camps, and similar police excesses. Invariably, the totalitarian system involves the utilization of unlimited police power. To avoid the perils of such a system is one of the major objectives of American constitutional law.

Furthermore, our system of criminal justice rests upon recognition of the fact that the contest in a criminal case is between parties of vastly unequal strength: a defendant, on the one hand, and government, on the other. Contemporary government is so powerful that legal safeguards are needed to protect the weaker party, since we know that inequality begets injustice. In addition, a very serious thing has happened to a person who is accused of a crime, wholly apart from the ultimate resolution of the issue of guilt or innocence. He may be imprisoned, pending trial; he may lose or be suspended from his job; his family relationships may be altered; his reputation is put under a cloud. Guilty or not, merely by virtue of an accusation a person is in deep trouble, and he must have every possible chance to combat the charges against him as quickly, as publicly, and as decisively as possible. Finally, and most fundamentally, the defendant's rights are important because we are convinced that if they are denied, justice will not be done. "It is not without significance," Justice Douglas has written, "that most of the provisions of the Bill of Rights are procedural. It is procedure that spells much of the difference between rule by law and rule by whim or caprice. Steadfast adherence to strict procedural safeguards is our main assurance that there will be equal justice under law."[3] Similarly, Justice Jackson once admonished that it should not be overlooked that due process of law is not for the sole benefit of the accused. "It is," he wrote, "the best insurance for the Government itself against those blunders which leave lasting stains on a system of justice but which are bound to occur on ex parte consideration."[4] It is not hyperbole to suggest, as Justice Frankfurter once observed, that "the history of American freedom is, in no small measure, the history of procedure."[5] While American judges are increasingly reluctant to hold, on substantive ground, that legislative bodies have overstepped the boundaries of a fair discretion, they are not at all reluctant to correct the other branches of government where considerations of procedural fairness are at stake, for, in the light of their professional knowledge and experience, they regard themselves as custodians of the principles of procedural fairness. As Justice Jackson once observed:

> Procedural due process is more elemental and less flexible than substantive due process. It yields less to the times, varies less with conditions, and defers less to legislative judgment. Insofar as it is technical law, it must be a specialized responsibility within the competence of the judiciary on which they do not bend before political branches of the Government, as they should on matters of policy which comprise substantive law.[6]

It is also worth noting that the apprehension, punishment, and deterrence of criminals is not the only objective of our criminal law. There are other important objectives which we regard as equally important, such as maintaining a decent respect for man's dignity and privacy and the preservation of an atmosphere of freedom. Most certainly, government efficiency in this area is not an end in itself, nor is it necessarily the highest good to be sought, for the plain truth is that it is possible to pay too high a price for efficiency. As Justice Rutledge wrote shortly before his death:

> Our government is not one of mere convenience or efficiency. It too has a stake, with every citizen, in his being afforded our historic individual protections, including those surrounding criminal trials. About them we dare not become careless or complacent when that fashion has become rampant over the earth.[7]

There can be no doubt that without the restraints of the law the police could apprehend and prosecutors could convict far more lawbreakers than they do now. For example, if the police had a completely free hand to break into any dwelling or other building, at any hour, to rummage around in the search for stolen goods and other contraband, unquestionably more crimes would be solved and more thieves, burglars, and dope peddlers put in jail. But the price we would have to pay, the utter destruction of all human privacy, would be prohibitively high. Similarly, if the police were free to torture suspects in order to secure confessions, the conviction rate would undoubtedly rise significantly, but again there are countervailing considerations, such as the danger of convicting innocent people who simply cannot endure the pain, and the even more dangerous consequence of brutalizing our police by permitting them to use uncivilized methods shocking to the conscience. As a matter of fact, 100 percent law enforcement is not a desirable objective of our system of criminal law. A distinguished legal scholar has challenged the validity of the objective by pointing out:

> The paradoxical fact is that arrest, conviction, and punishment of every criminal would be a catastrophe. Hardly one of us would escape, for we have all at one time or another committed acts that the law regards as serious offenses. Kinsey has tabulated our extensive sexual misdeeds. The Bureau of Internal Revenue is the great archive of our false swearing and cheating. The highway death toll statistics inadequately record our predilection for manslaughter. 100% law enforcement would not leave enough people at large to build and man the prisons in which the rest of us would reside.[8]

This observation is supported by the results of a survey made in behalf of the President's Commission on Law Enforcement and Administration of Justice, published in 1967, which indicated that in a sample of 1,700 persons, 91 percent of the respondents admitted to having committed acts for which they might have received jail or prison sentences.[9]

Clearly, in the field of criminal law enforcement a choice must be made between our desire to catch and punish lawbreakers and our concern for maintaining the legal amenities of a civilized community. In his memorable dissenting opinion in the original wiretapping case, Justice Holmes explained this point in language no one has since improved upon:

> We must consider two objects of desire, both of which we cannot have, and make up our minds which to choose. It is desirable that criminals should be detected, and to that end that all available evidence should be used. It also is desirable that the Government should not itself foster and pay for other crimes, when they are the means by which the evidence is to be obtained . . . We have to choose, and for my part I think it a less evil that some criminals should escape than that the Government should play an ignoble part.[10]

In the language of Justice Cardozo, expressed when he still served on the New York Court of Appeals, a criminal may go free because the constable blundered,[11] but this must be balanced off against a countervailing consideration, described by Justice Stewart as "the imperative of judicial integrity."[12] Similarly, in the opinion which extended the federal exclusionary rule to the states, Justice Clark drew attention to the competing considerations which must be kept in some sort of balanced state:

> Our decision, founded on reason and truth, gives to the individual no more than that which the Constitution guarantees him, to the police officer no less than that to which honest law enforcement is entitled, and, to the courts, that judicial integrity so necessary in the true administration of justice.[13]

Application of Federal Standards to State Courts

In the American federal system, both the national and state governments enact and enforce criminal laws. Except for such federal enclaves as the District of Columbia, over which Congress has plenary legislative authority, the power of the central government to define crimes is limited to its delegated and implied powers. Thus, federal criminal statutes are tied to such constitutional grants of legislative power as those relating to taxation, interstate commerce, and the postal system. Even so, the federal criminal code is a substantial body of statute law, and it is growing larger at an ever accelerating pace. Nevertheless, most of the criminal laws in the United States are state laws. The state is mainly responsible for the maintenance of law and order; most crimes are defined by state legislatures; and enforcement is in the hands of state police and judicial agencies. This is reflected in a quick comparison of state and federal prison populations. At the end of 1966, for example, adult felony offenders in state institutions numbered 180,409, whereas there were only 19,245 such persons in federal penal institutions.[14]

With rare exceptions,[15] federal criminal statutes are enforceable only in federal courts, and state courts enforce state criminal laws. In reviewing federal criminal cases, the Supreme Court not only gives effect to constitutional provisions relating to the rights of the accused, but also exercises general powers of supervision over the inferior federal courts,[16] in the same manner that a state supreme court exercises general appellate jurisdiction over its inferior courts. But the U.S. Supreme Court does not exercise general supervision over the state courts, for as Justice Harlan recently had occasion to point out, even the growing body of recent precedents does not establish the Court "as a rule-making organ for the promulgation of state rules of criminal procedure. And none of the specific provisions of the Constitution ordains this Court with such authority."[17] He stressed the point that so long as the challenged state's rules of evidence are not prohibited by any provision of the U.S. Constitution, there is nothing for the Supreme Court to review.[18] If a person has been convicted in a state trial court, and has taken and lost his appeal in the state's appellate courts, or has permitted his right of appeal to lapse, that is as far as he can go unless his appeal involves a substantial federal legal question. The U.S. Supreme Court does not sit to correct mere errors alleged to have occurred in state courts. "Our only power over state judgments," the Court has asserted, "is to correct them to the extent that they incorrectly adjudge federal rights."[19]

It is hornbook law that the provisions of the federal Bill of Rights, most of which are concerned with the rights of the accused, do not apply to the states.[20] The opening sentence of the First Amendment begins with the phrase "Congress shall make no law . . . ," and this would be curious language indeed if it had been intended to apply the provisions which followed as limitations upon state action. Thus, prior to the Civil War a defendant involved in a state criminal case had no way to get the U.S. Supreme Court, by way of appeal, to litigate any claim to any of the many defendant's rights spelled out in the federal Bill of Rights. Of course the adoption of the Fourteenth Amendment in 1868, with its provision that no state shall "deprive any person of life, liberty, or property, without due process of law," opened the door to an expanded federal review of state cases, but not for very long. As a consequence of restrictive, highly technical interpretations by the Supreme Court,[21] the various provisions of Section One of the Fourteenth Amendment got off to a very slow start. It was not until 1925 that the Court held that the "liberty" of the due process clause embraced the liberty of speech secured by the First Amendment,[22] and not until 1940 did the Court rule squarely that the First Amendment's guarantee of freedom of religion was part of the "liberty" which states are forbidden by the Fourteenth Amendment to deny to any person.[23]

The U.S. Supreme Court was for a long time extremely reluctant to review state appellate court decisions in criminal cases on due process grounds. As late as 1915, in **Frank v. Mangum,**[24] the Supreme Court refused to make an independent inquiry into the facts, holding that where a state has an appellate court authorized to correct errors, that court's review and affirmation of the conviction gave sufficient assurance that due process had not been denied. Speaking in dissent, Justices Holmes and Brandeis asserted that unless the federal court examines the facts, the right to due process will be "a barren one."[25] The principle of comity, which was so strenuously asserted in the Frank case, grounded in what would now seem to be an exaggerated respect for the state courts, was first abandoned in 1923, in the leading case of **Moore v. Dempsey.**[26] In this appeal, which also involved an allegation that the challenged conviction had been secured in a state trial court dominated by overwhelming mob pressures, Justice Holmes ruled that the federal district court, which had denied a petition for habeas corpus upon the state's demurrer, was obliged to make an independent investigation of the facts, even though the state's appellate court had ruled that a proper verdict had been reached on the basis of adequate evidence. ". . . If the case is," wrote Justice Holmes, "that the whole proceeding is a mask—that counsel, jury and judge were swept to the fatal end by an irresistible wave of public passion, and that the State Courts failed to correct the wrong, neither perfection in the machinery for correction nor the possibility that the trial court and counsel saw no other way of avoiding an immediate outbreak of the mob can prevent this Court from securing to the petitioners their constitutional rights."[27]

This seminal decision quickly led to an expansion of federal control over state administration of criminal law through review by the Supreme Court, the due process clause supplying the basic constitutional text. The meaning of due process, however, has been the subject of intense debate. The first Justice Harlan, who sat on the Court from 1877 to 1911,[28] and in our time Justices Black and Douglas[29] and some scholars,[30] have taken the position that the Fourteenth Amendment should be construed as nationalizing the whole federal Bill of Rights through the total incorporation of its provisions as federally enforceable limitations on the states. The theory of total incorporation, however, has never been accepted by a majority of the Justices, for they have preferred to follow a policy of selective incorporation.[31]

The first significant development following **Moore v. Dempsey** occurred in 1932, when, in the first Scottsboro case,[32] the Court ruled that a state has denied due process if it does not secure to a defendant, in a capital case, the right to counsel which is guaranteed to all defendants in federal courts by virtue of a specific provision in the Sixth Amendment. In 1963, the Court extended this doctrine to all serious cases, whether or not they involved capital offenses.[33] While the Court has declined to apply to the states those provisions of the Fifth Amendment which guarantee the right to indictment by grand jury,[34] most provisions of the Bill of Rights relating to the defendant's rights now apply as limitations upon the states, including the following: the federal concept of double jeopardy;[35] the Fourth Amendment right to be free from unreasonable searches and seizures, together with the ancillary right to have illegally seized evidence excluded from the trial;[36] the Fifth Amendment right to be free from compulsory self-incrimination;[37] the Sixth Amendment rights to counsel,[38] to a speedy trial,[39] to a public trial,[40] to confrontation of opposing witnesses,[41] and to compulsory process for obtaining witnesses;[42] and the Eighth Amendment's prohibition of cruel and unusual punishments.[43] This development reached some sort of climax in May, 1968, when the Court finally ruled that the Sixth Amendment guarantee of trial by jury applies to state criminal trials which involve serious, as distinguished from petty, crimes.[44]

The Supreme Court has employed various bits of rhetoric to explain why a right spelled out in the federal Bill of Rights should also be protected against state action through the Fourteenth Amendment. It has been asserted that the test is whether the right in question is among those "fundamental principles of liberty and justice which lie at the base of all our civil and political institutions,"[45] or whether it is a "basic in our system of jurisprudence,"[46] or whether it is "a fundamental right, essential to a fair trial."[47] In the recent case which held that the right to trial by jury is a due process right, the Court declared that it was "a protection against arbitrary rule."[48] These various tests are merely variations on the general theme that due process is a guarantee of justice and of a fair trial (as these concepts have acquired content in the course of historical experience).

In fact, the due process clause is not regarded as only a shorthand restatement of the federal Bill of Rights; it also has an independent force wholly outside its provisions. The Court has been quite willing to read the due process clause as including principles not mentioned in the

Bill of Rights at all. A very good illustration was the unanimous decision of the Court in 1960 which set aside a criminal conviction in a state court on the ground that there was no evidence in the record to support the conviction.[49] What the Court said, in effect, was that since it was wholly arbitrary and unreasonable for a state to convict and punish a man without evidence of guilt, such a capricious act violated the due process commitment of fundamental justice. This important decision soon became the basis for the overruling of many convictions for disturbing the peace and disorderly conduct which occurred as a result of the peaceful "sit-ins" which launched the contemporary civil rights movement in the South.[50]

Another illustration of a principle read into the due process clause which is wholly independent of the specific provisions of the federal Bill of Rights is the rule announced in 1935, in the celebrated **Mooney** case,[51] that a state has denied due process if the prosecution deliberately deceives the court and jury by the presentation of testimony known to be perjured. The court declared that this would be "as inconsistent with the rudimentary demands of justice as is the obtaining of a like result by intimidation."[52] Since this decision, the Court has on several occasions reversed a state conviction because of the knowing use of false testimony by the prosecution,[53] and indeed has extended the rule to include the suppression by the prosecution of evidence favorable to the accused.[54]

It is important to stress that when a state criminal case is appealed to the Supreme Court on the ground that a fundamental federal constitutional right is involved, the Court is not bound by the factual determinations of the state courts. For example, in the leading case of **Norris v. Alabama**,[55] which reversed the second convictions of the Scottsboro boys, this time because of the systematic and arbitrary exclusion of Negroes from jury service, Chief Justice Hughes wrote:

> That the question is one of fact does not relieve us of the duty to determine whether in truth a federal right has been denied. When a federal right has been specially set up and claimed in a state court, it is our province to inquire not merely whether it was denied in express terms but also whether it was denied in substance and effect. If this requires an examination of evidence, that examination must be made. Otherwise, review by this Court would fail of its purpose in safeguarding constitutional rights. Thus, whenever a conclusion of law of a state court as to a federal right and findings of fact are so intermingled that the latter control the former, it is incumbent upon us to analyze the facts in order that the appropriate enforcement of the federal right may be assured.[56]

This point is very well established in the jurisprudence of the Supreme Court.[57]

Basic Rights of the Defendant

Habeas Corpus

Since several lines of decisions of the Supreme Court have received most of the public's attention—such as those dealing with police interrogation, the right to counsel, compulsory self-incrimination, and unreasonable searches and seizures—many important decisions have gone unnoticed, except in professional circles. Recent cases relating to the uses of the writ of habeas corpus, for example, draw attention to the Court's willingness to expand the legal protections available to persons who have been convicted of crime. The federal habeas corpus statute speaks of giving relief to persons "in custody,"[58] and conventional wisdom has always held that the writ is available only if a person is actually restrained, since the only relief which the writ supplies is discharge from the restraint.[59] Nevertheless, a unanimous Court ruled in 1963 that a state prisoner who has been placed on parole is "in custody" within the meaning of the federal habeas corpus statute, because the terms of his parole impose significant restrictions upon his liberty.[60] Justice Black maintained that actual, physical custody was not always essential to give the habeas corpus court jurisdiction, that the writ does not supply "a static, narrow, formalistic remedy; its scope has grown to achieve its grand purpose—the protection of individuals against erosion of their right to be free from wrongful restraints upon their liberty."[61]

Similarly, a unanimous Court ruled in 1968 that a prisoner who was serving one of several consecutive sentences was entitled to petition for federal habeas corpus to attack a sentence which he was scheduled to serve in the future.[62] In so ruling the Court specifically rejected a 1934 precedent.[63] The decision turned on the proposition that postponement of adjudication hurts the petitioner, since memories grow dim and witnesses die, and the Court declared that the habeas corpus judge has discretion to fashion some remedy other than immediate release. A comparable ruling was made by a unanimous Court in 1968,[64] reversing a 5-4 decision arrived at in 1960,[65] to hold that if a prisoner in state custody applies for a federal writ, federal jurisdiction is not thereafter terminated because his sentence has expired and he has been discharged from parole status. The Court adopted the reasoning of the dissenting Justices in the earlier case, arguing that clearly the case was not moot because the petitioner still suffered from certain disabilities as a result of his conviction, the legality of which he attacked in his petition. He was unable to engage in certain businesses, such as a liquor business, he was ineligible for a period of time to serve as a labor union official, and he was not permitted to vote or serve as a juror in his state. Because of these collateral disabilities the Court held that the petitioner had a substantial stake in the judgment of conviction which survived the satisfaction of the sentence. Furthermore, Justice Fortas drew attention to the fact that the federal habeas corpus statute gives the Court a broad mandate in devising an appropriate form of relief, since the statute provides that "the court shall . . . dispose of the matter as law and justice require," and that it was amended by Congress in 1966 to authorize as relief "release from custody or other remedy."[66] Since the petitioner was continuing to suffer serious disabilities which would be unjustified if his claim to have been illegally convicted turned out to be meritorious, Justice Fortas could find "no need in the statute, the Constitution, or sound jurisprudence for denying to petitioner his ultimate day in court."[67]

One further recent change in federal habeas corpus law is worth noting. In 1950, in **Darr v. Burford,**[68] by a 5-3 vote, and in the teeth of a vigorous dissenting opinion by Justice Frankfurter, the Court ruled that if the petititioner is incarcerated under a state court judgment of conviction, a federal district court may not entertain his petition until all available state remedies have been exhausted, including a denial of certiorari review by the U.S. Supreme Court. In other words, under this rule a state prisoner was obliged to seek certiorari in the Supreme Court as a precondition for applying for federal habeas corpus in the U.S. district court. In 1963 the Court, by a 6-3 vote, decided to overrule the **Darr** case, pointing out that the Supreme Court is not a state court, and that unlike the writ of error, certiorari does not provide a normal appellate channel.[69] Justice Brennan also noted, as Justice Frankfurter had pointed out in 1950, that since most petitions for certiorari are denied, the **Darr** rule imposed an unnecessary burden on the petitioner and tended to clog the Court's calendar. Comity, Justice Brennan observed, "does not demand that such a price in squandered judicial resources be paid . . ."[70]

Trial by Jury

The willingness of the Court to abandon precedents is also reflected in recent decisions touching upon the right to trial by jury. Perhaps the most spectacular of all was the case of **Duncan v. Louisiana,**[71] decided in 1968, in which by a 7-2 vote the Supreme Court rejected the long-established rule that the due process clause of the Fourteenth Amendment does not require that state trials must be by jury.[72] The Court ruled that a state has violated due process if it refuses to grant the request of a defendant accused of a serious crime for trial by jury. In this case the accused was convicted of the crime of simple battery, which under Louisiana law is punishable by imprisonment for up to two years. The judge had denied the request on the stated ground that the Louisiana Constitution provides for jury trial only in cases in which capital punishment or imprisonment at hard labor may be imposed. The Supreme Court ruled that since trial by jury in criminal cases is fundamental to the American system of justice, and has impressive historical credentials going back to Magna Carta, it may not be denied by a state except in cases involving petty crimes or where jury trial has been waived. The Court held that a crime punishable by two years in jail must be regarded as a serious crime.

Characteristically, the Court declined to indicate just where the line should be drawn between petty and serious offenses, and thus this point remains to be worked out in future adjudication. But the **Duncan** decision poses other questions as well. One is whether a state is bound by the rule of unanimity which prevails in the federal courts. At least five states permit a conviction in criminal cases on less than a unanimous verdict.[73] Another question is whether a state is now free to have fewer than 12 persons on the jury. Many states employ juries with fewer than 12 members for certain types of criminal and civil cases. In short, does the fact that the federal Constitution now requires the state to offer jury trial to all persons accused of serious crime mean that the states must now conform with all aspects of the concept which prevails in the federal courts? It is a fair guess that this question will be answered by the Court some day, and that lawyers will soon be litigating these issues. In the meantime, one can only hazard the prediction that it is very doubtful that the Supreme Court will compel all states to observe a common pattern in an area where there has been so much variety and experimentation, and where the arguments for uniformity are so unconvincing.

The Court's attachment to the right of trial by jury is also reflected in recent decisions relating to criminal contempt proceedings. As recently as the **Barnett** case,[74] decided in 1964 by a 5-4 vote, the Court adhered to its traditional position that unless Congress has stipulated the right to trial by jury for specified contempts,[75] there is no right to jury trial in a proceeding for criminal contempt of court. The underlying theory was that a contempt proceeding was not a criminal prosecution within the meaning of the Sixth Amendment, and that the judge's power to punish for contempt was essential for the proper and effective administration of justice. In 1966, however, the Court ruled that a federal judge may not impose a sentence exceeding six months unless a jury trial has been received or waived.[76] The Court held that if the penalty is less than six months' incarceration, trial without jury would be appropriate, as it is in any case involving a petty offense. Finally, in 1968, the Court ruled squarely that a state court has violated due process by convicting a person of criminal contempt and sentencing him to jail for 24 months, after refusing a timely demand for a jury trial.[77] The Court reasoned that since serious contempts are like other serious crimes, they are within the jury provisions of the Constitution. It declared that criminal contempt is a crime in the ordinary sense of the term; it is a violation of law, a public wrong, punishable by fine or imprisonment, and the impact upon the individual is the same as in the case of any other crime. An even more compelling reason for jury trial in contempt cases was found in the fact that they often involve the judge's temperament, or a rejection of judicial authority, or an interference with judicial processes, the inference being that in such cases the judge may not be as detached and dispassionate as justice requires. Perhaps it should be noted here, however, that the Court has made it clear that there is no constitutionally protected right to jury trial in petty cases, as in a case involving a sentence of 10 days in jail,[78] or in civil as distinguished from criminal contempt proceedings.[79]

In addition, the Court has for some years been concerned with spelling out the elements inherent in the right to an impartial jury. While a closely divided Court has been able to reconcile this right with the presence on a federal jury of employees of the national government,[80] even in cases where Communists were defendants,[81] and while it has also held the New York "blue ribbon" jury system valid,[82] still the long campaign of the Court to protect the concept of a representative jury should not be minimized. Thus the Court's position has been that since the jury cannot be "the organ of any special group or class,"[83] the deliberate exclusion of any significant element of the community, such as daily wage earners,[84] does violence to the democratic nature of the jury system. Above all, in a long series of cases going back to the second Scottsboro case,[85] decided in 1935, the Court has established the position that a Negro defendant has been denied his Fourteenth Amendment right to the equal protection of the laws if he is put to trial under a jury system from which Negroes are systematically and arbitrarily excluded. Of course, this does not mean that a Negro is entitled to have a Negro jury, or that he has a right to have a number of Negroes on his jury which would be proportional to the Negro population of the district.[86] What he is entitled to is a jury system which does not exclude Negroes arbitrarily and systematically, and this applies to grand juries as well as trial juries.[87] Furthermore, where a large proportion of the population of the judicial district is Negro, and it is shown that for many years no Negro has ever served on a jury, the accused has established prima facie proof of forbidden discrimination, and the burden then shifts to the state to come forward with proof of its own, a mere denial or a bare assertion of proper intentions not being sufficient.

In 1968, the Court added a new dimension to the concept of jury impartiality when it set aside a death sentence imposed upon a defendant by an Illinois jury which had convicted him of murder.[89] An Illinois statute provided that in murder trials any prospective juror could be challenged for cause by the state if he asserted that he had conscientious scruples against or was opposed to capital punishment. This gave the prosecution unlimited challenges for cause to exclude jurors who, in the words of the Illinois Supreme Court, "might hesitate to return a verdict inflicting [death]."[90] At the trial the prosecution rejected nearly half of the venire of prospective jurors by challenges for cause, thus eliminating all who had expressed any qualms about capital punishment. Six Justices joined in ruling that this procedure denied the defendant the right to an impartial jury. They made it clear, however, that the case did not involve the right of the prosecution to challenge for cause those prospective jurors who assert that their reservations about capital punishment would prevent them from making an impartial decision on the issue of guilt. Nor did the excluded jurors say that they could never vote to impose the death penalty.

While future litigation will undoubtedly clarify the point, it would seem that the prosecution would have been within bounds if it had asked slightly different questions. Thus the Court concluded that by excluding those who merely said they were opposed to capital punishment, without more, the trial judge permitted the selection of a proper jury on the issue of guilt; but the Court ruled that on the issue of the penalty, the jury "fell woefully short" of that impartiality to which the accused was entitled. They maintained that on the issue of death the jury should express the conscience of the community, and since fewer than half of the American people believe in the death penalty, a jury composed exclusively of people who do accept it cannot speak for the community. In the Court's judgment, "the State produced a jury uncommonly willing to condemn a man to die."[91]

Finally, the Court's strong commitment to the jury system was dramatically reflected in another 1968 case in which the Court held one section of the Federal Kidnapping Act unconstitutional.[92] The statute provided that the offense was punishable by death only if the jury so recommended. The Court reasoned that this meant that the price the accused had to pay for asking for a jury trial was to risk being sentenced to death, since life imprisonment was the maximum penalty if jury trial was waived or if the accused pleaded guilty. Since the inevitable effect of the statute was to discourage the accused from requesting a jury trial, in the judgment of the Court it needlessly chilled the exercise of a basic constitutional right.

Right to Counsel

Another right which the Supreme Court takes very seriously is the right to counsel. The Court made up its mind in 1932, in the first Scottsboro case,[93] that at least in capital cases the right to counsel was secured by the due process clause of the Fourteenth Amendment. In noncapital cases the Court preferred to follow the rule that the denial of counsel by a state judge vitiated the proceedings only if there were special circumstances which resulted in injustice to the accused.[94] For a number of years the Court struggled with one case after another, trying to identify the special circumstances which would justify a reversal, including such factors as youth, inexperience, ignorance, mental inadequacy, complexity of the issues, or the occurrence of prejudicial errors resulting from the defendant's lack of counsel. In 1963, however, in **Gideon v. Wainwright,**[95] by a unanimous vote the Court reversed its position to hold that due process protects the right to counsel in noncapital as well as capital cases. Precedents, reason, and reflection, Justice Black said, "require us to recognize that in our adversary system of criminal justice, any person haled into court, who is too poor to hire a lawyer, cannot be assured of a fair trial unless counsel is provided for him." He noted that since the government, and defendants who have the money, engage lawyers, it is clear that in criminal cases lawyers are "necessities, not luxuries."

Having gone this far, the Court was confronted with the task of deciding just when, in the course of legal proceedings, the right to counsel accrues, and how long it continues. Within the last six years the Court has ruled that the accused has the right to the assistance of counsel at any in-custody interrogation following arrest,[96] at the police lineup held for eye-witness identification,[97] at a preliminary hearing if something critically important to the accused can happen there,[98] at his appeal,[99] and even at a posttrial proceeding for the revocation of probation.[100] In short, the rule today is that in all criminal proceedings, federal or state, except when petty offenses are involved,[101] the accused is entitled to representation by counsel at every stage where substantial rights may be affected.

At the time **Gideon** was decided, 13 states had current practices which were directly affected by the decision. It was authoritatively estimated at the time that of the 300,000 persons charged with felonies each year in the state courts, at least half could not afford to hire a lawyer.[102] Clearly, the new rule would require a considerable expenditure of money on the part of the states unless lawyers were required to give their services without compensation, a form of involuntary servitude now widely frowned upon. In addition, if the rule of the **Gideon** case was to be applied retroactively, a great many prisoners would have a chance to secure their freedom, at least until the state decided to retry them. The Supreme Court, for wholly unexplained reasons, did not rule expressly on the issue of retroactivity, although it reversed and remanded some 40 state criminal cases within the year following the decision in **Gideon.** The Florida courts quickly took the position that the **Gideon** rule was retroactive,[103] and "The results were spectacular. By January 1, 1964, nine hundred seventy-six prisoners had been released outright from Florida penitentiaries, the authorities feeling that they could not be successfully retried. Another five hundred were back in the courts, and petitions from hundreds more were awaiting consideration."[104]

In late February, 1964, the Supreme Court, in a two-sentence per curiam opinion, reversed a state criminal conviction which antedated **Gideon,**[105] and lower federal courts[106] and state appellate courts [107] were quick to rule that the **Gideon** principle was to be applied retroactively. Those who secured their freedom through a retroactive application of the **Gideon** rule, however, had to take their chances with second trials and the possibility of harsher sentences. Of the first batch of 300 Florida prisoners who were retried, most got off with reduced sentences—and12 were given longer sentences.[108] In a North Carolina case a prisoner who had been sentenced originally to a two-year term in jail, following a conviction for larceny, was sentenced to a 10-year term after a new trial.[109] The constitutionality of this sort of sentencing has been sharply challenged.[110] In any event, the impact of the **Gideon** decision has been enormous. Congress responded promptly with the enactment of the Criminal Justice Act of 1964[111] to provide more adequate representation of defendants in federal courts in all nonpetty cases, and within a two-year period, the legislatures and courts of 23 states had taken some specific action in response to the **Gideon** rule.[112]

Searches and Seizures

The most important recent development in the constitutional law relating to the freedom of the individual from unreasonable searches and seizures has been the application to the states of the federal exclusionary rule. In 1914 the Supreme Court ruled that evidence secured unlawfully had to be excluded by the federal trial judge, on motion of the defendant.[113] As late as 1949, after a full review, the Court refused to apply the exclusionary rule to the states as a requirement of due process.[114] In 1961, however, by a 5-4 vote, the Court ruled in **Mapp v. Ohio**[115] that the admission of unlawfully seized evidence by a state court violated due process, on the ground that exclusion was the only available remedy which would adequately safeguard the right in question, suits for damages and criminal prosecutions being woefully inadequate. In effect, the Court decided that no person should be convicted on unconstitutional evidence, whether in a federal or a state court. This decision, to which the Court has declined to give retroactive effect,[116] thus softening the blow, has had considerable impact upon the conduct of trials in the states, of which about half had continued to follow the old common law rule that relevant evidence is always admissible, no matter how it was secured.

Another aspect of search and seizure law which has recently received attention is the right of privacy in the home, which was weakened in 1959 when the Court, by a 5-4 vote, ruled that a health inspector may lawfully enter and search a private dwelling without a warrant if he has cause to believe that a nuisance exists in the house.[117] That a 5-4 decision in the delicate area of basic rights may have a short life expectancy is reflected in the fact that this decision was overruled eight years later,[118] the Court holding that administrative searches were "significant intrusions upon the interests protected by the Fourth Amendment,"[119] and that in the absence of an emergency situation, the preferable course is to require the inspector to secure a warrant, on a showing of probable cause, from a disinterested magistrate.

Finally, the Supreme Court has been struggling with the problem of electronic eavesdropping, though with mixed results. In 1967 the Court ruled that if federal agents attached an electronic listening and recording device to the outside of a public telephone booth, it was unlawful to permit testimony about the overheard conversations to be introduced as evidence at the trial.[120] The Court held that it was immaterial whether a telephone booth can be characterized as a constitutionally protected area, since the Fourth Amendment protects people and not places. It was felt that one who uses a public phone booth is entitled to assume that what he says will not be broadcast to the world. The absence of any element of trespass was also held to be immaterial. Even so, the Court ruled in this case that a magistrate could constitutionally have authorized such a search and seizure as this one with a proper warrant. This was made clear in **Berger v. New York,**[121] where the Court ruled out the use of evidence in a state trial which had been secured by placing a recording device in the defendant's office by virtue of a judge's order, pursuant to an authoriz-

ing statute. The Supreme Court did not rule out court-sanctioned eavesdropping, holding only that the New York procedure lacked the particu-
larization required by the Fourth Amendment. It was noted that the
judge's order was a broadside authorization which was not specific as to
the crime and the place and persons involved, and merely gave the officers
a roving commission. The inference was that electronic eavesdropping
is permissible if accomplished under adequate protective procedures and
judicial supervision. Congress responded quickly with the adoption of
Title III of the Omnibus Crime Control and Safe Streets Act of 1968.[122]
Amending Section 605 of the Communications Act, [123] the new statute
permits federal and state officers to wiretap and eavesdrop in a wide
range of specified cases, subject to detailed procedural requirements and
judicial supervision.

In actual fact, it has been very difficult to protect the sort of privacy
which is within the scope of the Fourth Amendment, for it is often flouted
with impunity. Changed police tactics can convert what might be regarded
as an illegally seized bit of property into "abandoned" property subject
to seizure outside the normal rules. No other constitutional right is violated so often, and with such an absence of popular resentment. Perhaps
part of the explanation lies in the fact that so many victims of unlawful
searches and seizures are the poor, the friendless, the unwanted, and the
unpopular—rarely the pillars of society. This is emphatically an area of
unfinished business in American law and practice.

Self-Incrimination

There can be no doubt that the Supreme Court has, since the beginning
of the Cold War period, strengthened the constitutional privilege against
compulsory self-incrimination. It ruled squarely, in 1964, that the due
process clause of the Fourteenth Amendment made the Fifth Amendment privilege applicable to the states to such a full extent that state
action must be judged by federal standards.[124] It held that since the
privilege is an essential mainstay of the American system of accusatorial
justice, it should make no difference whether a person is involved in a
federal or a state proceeding. In the same year the Court overruled several well-known precedents[125] to hold that a state witness cannot be compelled to give testimony which may be incriminating under federal law,[126]
thus catching up with an earlier holding that a witness in a federal court
may not be compelled to give testimony which could be used against him
in a state court.[127] Furthermore, since public stigma is often attached to
those who plead the privilege, and therefore they are driven to find ways

of claiming it in some evasive way or in ambiguous language, the Court has insisted that there is no particular verbal formula which must be employed in order to plead the privilege.[128] Its position is that tribunals must be alert to notice when the privilege is relied upon, even if it is not asserted in a direct and forthright way.

The Court has also made it abundantly clear that the privilege extends not only to testimony which actually incriminates the witness directly, but also to any testimony which may tend to incriminate, that is to say, any evidence which will supply a link in the chain of evidence that may lead to a criminal conviction.[129] This explains why it is lawful for an individual to refuse to admit membership in the Communist party; although such membership is not illegal per se, an admission of this sort could be used as evidence to prosecute for violation of the sedition laws. It was on this ground that the Court invalidated a statute which required Communists to register with the attorney general.[130] Similarly, the Court has held invalid federal statutes which had the effect of requiring certain persons to admit, through a process of registration, that they were gamblers,[131] or, when registering certain weapons, that they engaged in certain unlawful activities.[132] Equally suggestive are holdings which forbid the dismissal of a teacher[133] or a police officer,[134] or the disbarment of a lawyer,[135] merely because the individual invoked the privilege against self-incrimination. Similar reasoning was employed by the Court in 1965, when it decided that if a state permits the judge or prosecutor to invite the jury to make an unfavorable inference by commenting on the defendant's silence, "it cuts down on the privilege by making its assertion costly," in violation of due process.[136]

The significance which the Supreme Court attaches to the right to be free from compulsory self-incrimination was underscored in 1966 in **Miranda v. Arizona.**[137] Perhaps its critics exaggerated the impact this case would have upon police activity, but it has clearly been the most widely discussed of the Court's recent decisions. In this case the Court held that in all federal and state criminal proceedings, once the accused is in custody, he may not be interrogated by police officers unless he is first warned that he has a right to remain silent, that any statement he makes may be used against him, and that he has a right to the presence of a lawyer, retained or appointed. The **Miranda** rules state that the accused may waive these rights, provided that the waiver is made voluntarily, knowingly, and intelligently. Furthermore, if at any time in the course of the questioning he indicates that he wishes to consult an attorney, there can be no more questioning; and if the accused is alone and indicates in any manner that he does not wish to be interrogated, the police may not question him. The mere fact that he has answered some questions or has on his own volunteered some statements does not deprive him of the right to refrain from responding to any further questions until he has consulted with a lawyer, and thereafter consents to be questioned. Only by observing these rules, said Chief Justice Warren for a bare majority of the Court, is it possible to protect a privilege which is so essential for the adversary system of justice and for protecting the dignity and integrity of the individual. It was also noted that police officers may ask questions freely of a person who is not under restraint, and that statements made freely and voluntarily are not barred.

It is worth noting that the Court did not create the **Miranda** rules in some quick flash of creative inspiration. As long ago as 1943 the Court ruled that statements made by the accused during a period of illegal detention are inadmissible.[138] By 1964, in the **Escobedo** case, [139] the Court had reached the point where it was willing to set aside a conviction because the police persisted in questioning a person in custody after refusing his request to consult with his lawyer, who was just outside the door. Furthermore, the **Miranda** rules were fully in accord with well-established English law,[140] with the law and practice of some of the states,[141] and with the going practices of such federal law enforcement agencies as the FBI, which, as Chief Justice Warren noted in his **Miranda** opinion, has over the years "compiled an exemplary record of effective law enforcement" while observing such rules.[142] Finally, the Court soon ruled that the **Miranda** decision was not retroactive.[143]

When the **Miranda** decision was announced, it was widely criticized by police officials and prosecutors on the ground that it would interfere with law enforcement by inhibiting the solution of crimes through the confession route. It quickly developed that there was very little solid information available on the extent to which convictions depended upon confessions, and it was pointed out by experienced officers that the average criminal never would talk to the police in any event. A quick survey by the District Attorney of the County of Los Angeles demonstrated that "confessions are essential to a successful prosecution in only a small percentage of criminal cases," and that "the percentage of cases in which confessions or admissions were made has not decreased, as might have been anticipated, because of the increased scope of the admonitions required by **Miranda**."[144] Milwaukee police statistics indicated that in 1965, a pre-**Miranda** year, the police cleared up 55 percent of the burglaries and 64 percent of the robberies, while in the first full year after **Miranda,** 1967, the burglary solution rate fell to 41 percent, but the robbery rate rose to 80 percent, leading a top prosecutor in the district attorney's office to comment, "I have no quarrel with **Miranda** whatever."[145] A local judge who had once served as district attorney in Milwaukee also pointed out that those experienced criminals who do not make confessions or incriminating statements under **Miranda** conditions would have remained silent even in the absence of such rules. He also observed that "any legal procedures which acquaint a potential defendant with his rights have salutary features."

A unique study made by some Yale Law School students during the summer of 1966, involving 24-hour observation over a period of 11 weeks and a great deal of interviewing, led to the conclusion that there was no evidence which indicated that the **Miranda** warnings caused many suspects to refuse to talk or to request counsel.[146] It was also found that questioning was necessary to solve crimes in less than 10 percent of the felony cases in which an arrest was made, and that of the 127 suspects whose interrogations were witnessed, only six were possibly affected adversely by the operation of the **Miranda** rules. The net conclusion reached was that "not much has changed after **Miranda**," and two main reasons for this were cited. First, at least in a middle-sized city like New Haven, interrogations play only a secondary role in solving crimes, "both because serious offenses are relatively infrequent and because the police rarely arrest suspects without substantial evidence." Second, the **Miranda** rules seem to affect interrogations only slightly. "The police continue to question suspects, and succeed despite the new constraints." The explanation for this seems to lie in the fact that the atmosphere of a police station is inherently coercive, and the suspect is "in a crisis-laden situation," all of which leads him to try to talk his way out of his difficulty, in the hope for leniency. Furthermore, "as long as the police question the suspect alone, he is no match for them."[147]

Other studies of the impact of **Miranda** have yielded similar observations. A comparison of police records in Pittsburgh for the first six months after **Miranda** with a similar previous period led to the generalization that "**Miranda** has not impaired significantly the ability of law enforcement agencies to apprehend and convict the criminal."[148] A study of custodial police interrogation in the District of Columbia reached the same general conclusions which the Yale study yielded,[149] and a study based upon questionnaires distributed nationally to prosecutors and police officers concluded with the observation that the police are unable "to carry out policies in a meaningful way when the means for implementation are largely left to them."[150] What is most needed, the author argued, is a serious revision of the system of law enforcement, with city officials and prosecutors playing a decisive role, to the end that "the police are seen as the instrument rather than the creator of policy . . . ."[151]

Right to a Fair Trial

In addition to all of the specific guarantees of defendants' rights which are spelled out in the Bill of Rights, due process of law in its most seminal aspect secures to all who are accused of crime the benefits of a fair trial. The concept of a fair trial is a broad and a generous one, and has been developing in all its many facets over centuries. The Supreme Court has, in our day, expanded and deepened the concept in many different ways. To mention but a few holdings, merely to illustrate the point, the Court has ruled that a state juvenile code offends the Constitution by denying the juvenile offender such due process rights as adequate written notice of specific charges, the right of confrontation, the right to counsel, and the privilege against self-incrimination.[152] Justice Fortas declared that the history of the juvenile court idea has demonstrated "that unbridled discretion, however benevolently motivated, is frequently a poor substitute for principle and procedure," and he added that "under our Constitution, the condition of being a boy does not justify a kangaroo court."[153]

There are many ingredients of a fair hearing which have received serious attention in recent years, such as the right to have all the evidence bearing upon the central issue of guilt or innocence presented to the jury in court, and in no other way,[154] the right to confront one's accusers and hostile witnesses, and to cross-examine them,[155] the right to inspect reports previously made to the police by informer-witnesses,[156] the right to a public trial [157] and a speedy trial[158] in state as well as federal courts, the right of the accused to be protected by the trial judge against the consequences of inherently prejudicial publicity which had saturated the community,[159] the right to be tried in a proper atmosphere, free from the distractions of unwanted television broadcasting,[160] the right to have adequate notice of prohibited conduct,[161] the right to a hearing on the issue of mental competence to stand trial,[162] the right to be heard on any charge which the judge makes a basis for sentencing,[163] and the right of the accused in a state court to have compulsory process for obtaining witnesses in his favor.[164] Clearly the right to a fair trial holds a prominent and growing place in the concept of due process, which in the jurisprudence of the Supreme Court is as applicable to state as to federal practices.

The Indigent Defendant

Finally, since 1956, the Court has displayed unusual interest in the problems with which the poor are confronted when they become involved in the process of the criminal law. On the premise that, taken together, due process and the guarantee of equal protection of the laws call for procedures in criminal trials which allow no invidious discrimination between persons and groups, and that "in criminal trials a State can no more discriminate on account of poverty than on account of religion, race, or color," the Supreme Court ruled that Illinois had violated the Fourteenth Amendment in refusing to give an indigent defendant who had been convicted of armed robbery a free transcript of the trial proceedings.[165] Under Illinois law, in order to secure full, direct review of alleged errors by writ of error, it is necessary for the defendant to furnish the appellate court with a bill of exceptions, and the state conceded that sometimes it is impossible to prepare a bill of exceptions without a transcript. Further, the state law provided for a free transcript at county expense if the indigent defendant was sentenced to death or if he raised constitutional questions in his appeal. The Supreme Court ruled that an indigent defendant has been denied his federal rights if he is denied a free transcript because he alleged only nonconstitutional legal errors. It was conceded that a state is not required by the Constitution to provide for appellate review at all, but if it does, then it is forbidden to discriminate against a defendant because of his poverty. Since many convictions are reversed by state appellate courts, the refusal of adequate review to the poor means that they are denied the same opportunity that others have to get appellate courts to set aside unjust convictions. "There can be no equal justice," Justice Black declared, "where the kind of trial a man gets depends on the amount of money he has."[166]

The decision which opened a new door to the expansion of protection for the poor who are involved with the criminal law was sharply challenged by four members of the Court. Justice Burton argued that "Illinois is not bound to make the defendants economically equal before its bar of justice,"[167] that while it may be desirable social policy for a state to do so, it is not a command of the Constitution. In another dissenting opinion, Justice Harlan pointed out that only 29 states then provided free transcripts as of right to indigents convicted of noncapital crimes, and that the sweeping new pronouncement would create many problems regarding the status of an unknown multitude of indigent convicts.

These considerations did not deter the Court from the path upon which it embarked in 1956. Thus, the Court soon ruled, in a series of cases, that a state violates the Constitution by giving an indigent defendant a transcript at public expense only if the judge believes that justice will thereby be promoted,[168] or only if the judge finds that assignments of error were not frivolous,[169] and by refusing a free transcript in a coram nobis proceeding merely because the indigent defendant insisted upon appearing without a lawyer.[170] Similarly, the Court has emphasized that federal courts must be careful to give poor defendants adequate trans-

cripts in order to take appeals.[171] In addition, the Court has decided that
a state may not refuse an indigent defendant leave to appeal,[172] or a
chance to apply for habeas corpus,[173] because he cannot pay filing or
docket fees. Finally, in 1962 the Court ruled that when one who has been
convicted in a federal court applies for leave to appeal in forma pauperis,
the burden is on the government to prove that the appeal is frivolous.[174]
Said Chief Justice Warren:

> When society acts to deprive one of its members of his life, liberty or
> property, it takes its most awesome steps. No general respect for, nor
> adherence to, the law as a whole can well be expected without judicial
> recognition of the paramount need for prompt, eminently fair and sober
> criminal law procedures. The methods we employ in the enforcement of
> our criminal law have aptly been called the measures by which the
> quality of our civilization may be judged.[175]

Why the Court's Attitude?

The Chief Justice's remarks supply an appropriate comment with which
to close this discussion of rights of the accused in the jurisprudence of
the Court over which he presides. While it is by no means true that all
defendants have won their appeals in this court,[176] on the whole it is quite
clear that the Justices have been pushing steadily in the direction of
strengthening the defendant's position. In doing so, they have been willing
to overrule precedents, many of which enjoyed the venerability which
comes with age, and to chart new rules of law. Unquestionably these
decisions have had impact upon the states, which still carry the principal
burden in the enforcement of the criminal law. Many of the Court's
decisions go far beyond mere negation and require the states to do positive
things, such as admitting Negroes to service on juries, or providing for
jury trial in all serious cases. Some of these decisions require the states
to do things that cost money, such as supplying attorneys or transcripts
to indigent defendants. Of course, these decisions do not always meet
with quick and general approval, and state officials and judges are quite
capable of dragging their feet so far as compliance is concerned, as in the
case of the local resistance to the exclusionary rule;[177] but if the Court
persists, and clarifies its original position in later decisions, the long-run
tendency seems to be in the direction of acceptance of the new federal
rules of law.

Of course, where so much law is changed in such a short period of
time, there are bound to be complaints and criticisms. Many police officials have been outspoken in expressing their opposition to the Court's
decisions in the criminal law field. Speaking to the Judicial Conference

of the Third Judicial Circuit on September 9, 1965, Michael Murphy, former Police Commissioner of New York City, gave expression to views widely held in law enforcement circles when he said:

> It is my firm conclusion that recent Supreme Court decisions have unduly hampered—and will in the future further hamper—the administration of criminal justice. . . . Police are not alone in their conclusion that we are reaching a critical stage in our never-ending search for the illusive balance between the needs of the community and the rights of the individual.[178]

In fact, such views are also expressed by some members of the Supreme Court. Thus, in his dissenting opinion in **Escobedo,**[179] Justice White remarked:

> I do not suggest for a moment that law enforcement will be destroyed by the rule announced today. The need for peace and order is too insistent for that. But it will be crippled and its task made a great deal more difficult, all in my opinion, for unsound, unstated reasons, which can find no home in any of the provisions of the Constitution.

It is very difficult to believe that the Justices have been animated by any puerile sentimentality or softness about criminals, or that they have been trying to create loopholes through which criminals may escape the consequences of their offenses against society. Nor is there any reason to believe that the Justices have been unaware of the seriousness of the crime problem, or indifferent to the community's need for orderly and lawful human relations. They have been trying to find a balance between the needs of society and the rights of an individual who is caught up in an adversary situation where he is the weaker party. They have been animated by the overriding purpose of promoting justice, which is the great end of government. Of course, the guarantees for defendants help them, but in a larger sense they help our society do right and avoid injustice. The balance is difficult to define, and is never stationary or perfect. As conditions change, and as human perceptions about the requirements of justice change, so the law changes.

That there has been so much change in the United States in recent years in respect to the rights of the defendant accused of crime is testimony to the fact that American public law is resilient and sensitive to the requirements of a dynamic society which is static neither with respect to objective conditions nor in regard to conceptions of justice. There is no ultimate, final solution; what matters most is that inquiry and adjustment should continue freely in the search for tolerable levels of balance. In this search the Supreme Court has moved carefully, deciding one case at a time, and always within the general body of American legal tradition.

As the former Solicitor General of the United States, Archibald Cox, remarked at the conclusion of his recent lectures on the Warren Court:

> Only history will know whether the Warren Court has struck the balance right. For myself, I am confident that historians will write that the trend of decisions during the 1950's and 1960's was in keeping with the mainstream of American history—a bit progressive but also moderate, a bit humane but not sentimental, a bit idealistic but seldom doctrinaire, and in the long run essentially pragmatic—in short, in keeping with the true genius of our institutions.[180]

Notes

1. See the remarks of Lord Chief Justice Reading in R. V. Shama (1914) 79 J.P. 184; 24 Cox C.C. 591; 11 Cr. App. R. 45 (C.C.A.). Cf. comments Justice Frankfurter in Leland v. Oregon. 343 U.S. 790, 802-03 (1952) (dissenting opinion). See also Abraham S. Goldstein, "The State and the Accused: Balance of Advantage in Criminal Procedure," *Yale Law Journal,* LXIX (June, 1960), 1149-99.

2. Watts v. Indiana, 338 U.S. 49, 54 (1949).

3. Joint Anti-Fascist Committee v. McGrath, 341 U.S. 123, 179 (1951) (concurring opinion).

4. Shaughnessy v. United States *ex rel.* Mezei, 345 U.S. 206, 224-25 (1953) (dissenting opinion).

5. Malinski v. New York, 324 U.S. 401, 414 (1945) (concurring opinion).

6. Shaughnessy v. United States *ex rel.* Mezei, supra.

7. Kotteakos v. United States, 328 U.S. 750, 773 (1946).

8. Louis B. Schwartz, "On Current Proposals to Legalize Wire Tapping," *University of Pennsylvania Law Review,* CIII (1954), 157-67, see 157.

9. The President's Commission on Law Enforcement and Administration of Justice, *The Challenge of Crime in a Free Society* (Washington, D.C.: U.S. Government Printing Office, 1967), p. v.

10. Olmstead v. United States, 277 U.S. 438, 470 (1928).

11. People v. Defore, 242 N.Y. 13, 21; 150 N.E. 585, 587 (1926).

12. Elkins v. United States, 364 U.S. 206, 222 (1960).

13. Mapp v. Ohio, 367 U.S. 643, 659 (1961).

14. Bureau of Prisons, U.S. Department of Justice, *Prisoners in State and Federal Institutions for Adult Felons, 1966.*

15. Testa v. Katt, 330 U.S. 386 (1947). During World War II, in its desire to enlist all the judicial power in the country to enforce price control legislation, Congress required the state courts to help enforce the federal statutes. At the present time no federal criminal statute is enforceable in a state court.

16. McNabb v. United States, 318 U.S. 332, 341 (1943): "The principles governing the admissibility of evidence in federal criminal trials have not been restricted . . . to those derived solely from the Constitution. In the exercise of its supervisory authority over the administration of criminal justice in the federal courts, . . . this Court has, from the very beginning of its history, formulated rules of evidence to be applied in federal criminal prosecutions."

17. Spencer v. Texas, 385 U.S. 554, 564 (1967).

18. Idem at 568-69.

19. Herb v. Pitcairn, 324 U.S. 117, 125-26 (1945).

20. Barron v. Baltimore, 7 Pet. (U.S.) 243 (1833).

21. See, e.g., Slaughter-House Cases, 16 Wall. (U.S.) 36 (1873); Civil Rights Cases, 109 U.S. 3 (1883).

22.   Gitlow v. New York, 268 U.S. 652 (1925).

23.   Cantwell v. Connecticut, 310 U.S. 296 (1940).

24.   237 U.S. 309.

25.   Idem at 348.

26.   261 U.S. 86.

27.   261 U.S. 91.

28.   See his dissenting opinions in Hurtado v. California, 110 U.S. 516 (1884); Maxwell v. Dow, 176 U.S. 581 (1900); Twining v. New Jersey, 211 U.S. 78 (1908).

29.   See the dissenting opinion of Justice Black in Adamson v. California, 332 U.S. 46, 68 (1947).

30.   See Horace E. Flack, *The Adoption of the Fourteenth Amendment* (Baltimore: Johns Hopkins University Press, 1908); Joseph B. James, *The Framing of the Fourteenth Amendment* (Urbana: University of Illinois Press, 1956).

31.   The leading scholarly defense of the Court's position is Charles Fairman, "Does the Fourteenth Amendment Incorporate the Bill of Rights? The Original Understanding," *Stanford Law Review*, II (December, 1949), 5-139.

32.   Powell v. Alabama, 287 U.S. 45 (1932).

33.   Gideon v. Wainwright, 372 U.S. 335 (1963).

34.   Hurtado v. California, 110 U.S. 516 (1884).

35.   Benton v. Maryland, 39 U.S. 784 (1969), overruling Palko v. Connecticut, 302 U.S. 319 (1937).

36.   Mapp v. Ohio, 367 U.S. 643 (1961).

37.   Malloy v. Hogan, 378 U.S. 1 (1964).

38.   Gideon v. Wainwright, 372 U.S. 335 (1963).

39.   Klopfer v. North Carolina, 386 U.S. 213 (1967).

40.   In re Oliver, 333 U.S. 257 (1948).

41.   Pointer v. Texas, 380 U.S. 400 (1965).

42.   Washington v. Texas, 388 U.S. 14 (1967).

43.   Robinson v. California, 370 U.S. 660 (1962).

44.   Duncan v. Louisiana, 391 U.S. 145 (1968).

45.   Powell v. Alabama, 287 U.S. 45, 67 (1932).

46.   In re Oliver, 333 U.S. 257, 273 (1948).

47.   Gideon v. Wainwright, 372 U.S. 335, 343-44 (1963); Malloy v. Hogan, 378 U.S. 1, 6 (1964); Pointer v. Texas, 380 U.S. 400, 403 (1965).

48.   Duncan v. Louisiana, 391 U.S. 145, 149, 151 (1968).

49.   Thompson v. Louisville, 362 U.S. 199 (1960).

50.   See Garner v. Louisiana, 368 U.S. 157 (1961); Taylor v. Louisiana, 370 U.S. 154 (1962); Barr v. Columbia, 378 U.S. 146 (1964); Shuttlesworth v. Birmingham, 382 U.S. 87 (1965); Johnson v. Florida, 20 L. Ed. 2d 838 (1968). In all these cases, state convictions were set aside on the ground that there was no evidence in the record to support the results.

51.   Mooney v. Holohan, 294 U.S. 103 (1935).

52.   Idem at 112.

53.   Mesarosh v. United States, 352 U.S. 1 (1956); Alcorta v. Texas, 355 U.S. 28 (1957); Miller v. Pate, 386 U.S. 1 (1967).

54.   Brady v. Maryland, 373 U.S. 83 (1963); Giles v. Maryland, 386 U.S. 66 (1967).

55.   294 U.S. 580 (1935).

56.   Idem at 589-90.

57.   Fiske v. Kansas, 274 U.S. 380, 385 (1927); Chambers v. Florida, 309 U.S. 227, 228-29 (1940); Ashcraft v. Tennessee, 322 U.S. 143, 147-48 (1944); Craig v. Harney, 331 U.S. 378, 373 (1947).

58. 28 U.S.C. 2241 (c) (3) (1964).

59. Wales v. Whitney, 114 U.S. 564, 571-72 (1885): "Something more than moral restraint is necessary to make a case for habeas corpus. There must be actual confinement or the present means of enforcing it." Thus, if the accused is free on bail, he cannot use the writ to secure a judicial inquiry into the size of the bail, not being in custody. Johnson v. Hoy, 227 U.S. 245 (1913).

60. Jones v. Cunningham, 371 U.S. 236 (1963). The petitioner had to live with a specified aunt and uncle, could not leave the community, or change his residence, or operate a motor vehicle without the permission of his parole officer, and was obliged to report to his parole officer once a month.

61. Idem at 243.

62. Peyton v. Rowe, 391 U.S. 54 (1968). Cf. Walker v. Wainwright, 390 U.S. 335 (1968), holding that a prisoner may test his current detention even though another prison term might await him if he should succeed in establishing the illegality of his present imprisonment.

63. McNally v. Hill, 293 U.S. 131 (1934).

64. Carafas v. LaVallee, 391 U.S. 234 (1968).

65. Parker v. Ellis, 362 U.S. 574 (1960).

66. 28 U.S.C. §2244 (b) (1964 ed., Supp. II).

67. 391 U.S. at 239.

68. 339 U.S. 200.

69. Fay v. Noia, 372 U.S. 391 (1963).

70. 372 U.S. at 437.

71. 391 U.S. 145.

72. The leading precedents were Walker v. Sauvinet, 92 U.S. 92 (1876); and Maxwell v. Dow, 176 U.S. 581 (1900).

73. Harry Kalven, Jr., and Hans Zeisel, *The American Jury* (Boston: Little, Brown, 1966), p. 461. For crimes below the grade of felony, or in criminal cases tried in inferior courts, a conviction may be had in Idaho by a five-sixths vote, in Montana by a two-thirds vote, and in Oklahoma by a three-fourths vote. In noncapital cases a vote of nine is sufficient to convict in Louisiana, and 10 in Oregon. Many states permit nonunanimous verdicts in civil cases. In Miss. & St. Louis R.R. Co. v. Bombolis, 241 U.S. 211 (1916), the Court ruled that the federal unanimity rule does not control the state courts even where they are enforcing a right under a federal statute.

74. United States v. Barnett, 376 U.S. 681 (1964). This issue was fully reviewed in Green v. United States, 356 U.S. 165 (1958). Justice Clark cited some 50 precedents which supported this view. 376 U.S. at 694.

75. See, e.g., Michaelson v. United States, 266 U.S. 43 (1924).

76. Cheff v. Schnackenberg, 384 U.S. 373 (1966).

77. Bloom v. Illinois, 391 U.S. 194 (1968).

78. Dyke v. Taylor Implement Mfg. Co., 391 U.S. 216 (1968).

79. Shillitani v. United States, 384 U.S. 364 (1966).

80. United States v. Wood, 299 U.S. 123 (1936); Frazier v. United States, 335 U.S. 497 (1948).

81. Dennis v. United States, 339 U.S. 162 (1950).

82. Fay v. New York, 332 U.S. 261 (1947); Moore v. New York, 333 U.S. 565 (1948). The vote in both cases was 5-4.

83. Glasser v. United States, 315 U.S. 60, 86 (1942).

84. Thiel v. Southern Pacific Co., 328 U.S. 217 (1946).

85. Norris v. Alabama, 294 U.S. 587 (1935). The point was first made in Strauder v. West Virginia, 100 U.S. 303 (1880). The Civil Rights Act of March 1, 1875, 18 Stat. 335, 18 U.S.C. § 243, makes it a federal crime for state officials to discriminate against Negroes in regard to jury service, but prosecutions are extremely rare; the

principal federal weapon has been the power of the Supreme Court to reverse a conviction or set aside an indictment of a Negro who has been tried or indicted in a state court which practiced racial discrimination.

86. Akins v. Texas, 325 U.S. 398 (1945).

87. Pierre v. Louisiana, 306 U.S. 354 (1939).

88. Patton v. Mississippi, 332 U.S. 463 (1947).

89. Witherspoon v. Illinois, 391 U.S. 510 (1968).

90. People v. Carpenter, 13 Ill. 2d 470, 476; 150 N.E. 2d 100, 103 (1958).

91. The three dissenting Justices protested that the Court was making it impossible for a state to get a jury which, under these rules, will enforce the death penalty, and that it was not up to the Court to decide whether the death penalty should be abolished.

92. United States v. Jackson, 390 U.S. 570 (1968).

93. Powell v. Alabama, 387 U.S. 45 (1932).

94. The leading case was Betts v. Brady, 316 U.S. 455 (1942).

95. 372 U.S. 335. See Anthony Lewis, *Gideon's Trumpet* (New York: Random House, 1964).

96. Escobedo v. Illinois, 378 U.S. 478 (1964); Miranda v. Arizona, 384 U.S. 436 (1966).

97. United States v. Wade, 388 U.S. 218 (1967); Gilbert v. California, 388 U.S. 263 (1967).

98. Hamilton v. Alabama, 368 U.S. 52 (1961); White v. Maryland, 373 U.S. 59 (1963).

99. Douglas v. California, 372 U.S. 353 (1963); Anders v. California, 386 U.S. 738 (1967); Entsminger v. Iowa, 386 U.S. 748 (1967).

100. Mempa v. Rhay, 389 U.S. 128 (1967).

101. For example, the New York Court of Appeals has ruled that the right cannot be claimed by one who is charged with such a petty offense as a traffic offense. People v. Letterio, 16 N.Y. 2d 307; 266 N.Y.S. 2d 368; 213 N.E. 2d 670 (1965); cert. denied, 384 U.S. 911 (1966). On the other hand, the Supreme Court of Minnesota has decided that the right to counsel applies to indigent misdemeanor offenders who may be given any jail sentence. State v. Borst, 278 Minn. 388; 154 N.W. 2d 888 (1967).

102. Lee Silverstein, *Defense of the Poor,* Vol. I, *National Report* (Chicago: American Bar Foundation, 1965), 7.

103. King v. State, 157 So. 2d 440 (Fla. App. 1963); Geather v. State, 165 So. 2d 229 (Fla. App. 1964).

104. Lewis, op. cit., p. 205.

105. Doughty v. Maxwell, 376 U.S. 202 (1964).

106. Palumbo v. New Jersey, 334 F. 2d 524 (3d Cir. 1964); U.S. ex rel. Durocher v. LaValee, 330 F. 2d 303 (2d Cir. 1964), cert. denied, 377 U.S. 980 (1964); U.S. ex rel. Craig v. Myers, 220 F. Supp. 762 (E.D. Penna. 1963), aff'd., 329 F. 2d 856 (3d Cir. 1964).

107. State ex rel. May v. Boles, 139 S.E. 2d 177 (W. Va. 1964); Com. ex rel. McCray v. Rundle, 415 Pa. 65, 202 A. 2d 303 (1964); Manning v. State, 237 Md. 349, 206 A. 2d 563 (1965).

108. G. Theodore Mitau, *Decade of Decision* (New York: Charles Scribner's Sons, 1967), p. 161.

109. State v. Williams, 261 N.C. 172, 134 S.E. 2d 163 (1964).

110. William W. Van Alstyne, "In Gideon's Wake: Harsher Penalties and the 'Successful' Criminal Appellant," *Yale Law Journal,* LXXIV (March, 1965), 606-39.

111. 78 Stat. 552.

112. Mitau, op. cit., p. 161. On the costs involved see Silverstein, op. cit., Ch. 4.

113. Weeks v. United States, 232 U.S. 383 (1914). Later the Court extended the exclusionary rule to apply to evidence which, though not seized unreasonably, was secured as a consequence of an unlawful seizure. Silverthorne Lumber Co. v. United States, 251 U.S. 385 (1920).

114. Wolf v. Colorado, 338 U.S. 25 (1949).

115. 367 U.S. 643.

116. Linkletter v. Walker, 381 U.S. 618 (1965).

117. Frank v. Maryland, 359 U.S. 360 (1959). An equally divided Court took the same position in Eaton v. Price, 364 U.S. 263 (1960).

118. Camara v. Municipal Court of San Francisco, 387 U.S. 523 (1967); See v. City of Seattle, 387 U.S. 541 (1967). Three Justices dissented in these cases, taking the position that no warrant was required for inspection under municipal fire, health, or housing inspection programs.

119. 387 U.S. at 534.

120. Katz v. United States, 389 U.S. 347 (1967).

121. 388 U.S. 41 (1967).

122. 82 Stat. 211.

123. See Nardone v. United States, 302 U.S. 379 (1937); Lee v. Florida, 393 U.S. 378 (1968), overruling Schwartz v. Texas, 344 U.S. 199 (1952).

124. Malloy v. Hogan, 378 U.S. 1 (1964).

125. The following precedents were specifically overruled: United States v. Murdock, 284 U.S. 141 (1931); Knapp v. Schweitzer, 357 U.S. 371 (1958); Feldman v. United States, 322 U.S. 487 (1944).

126. Murphy v. Waterfront Commission of New York, 378 U.S. 52 (1964). Cf. Elkins v. United States, 364 U.S. 207 (1960), which held that evidence seized illegally by state officials may not be received in a federal court.

127. United States v. The Saline Bank of Virginia, 1 Pet. (U.S.) 100 (1828).

128. Quinn v. United States, 349 U.S. 155 (1955); Emspak v. United States, 349 U.S. 190 (1955).

129. Patricia Blau v. United States, 340 U.S. 159 (1950).

130. Albertson v. Subversive Activities Control Board, 382 U.S. 70 (1965).

131. Marchetti v. United States, 390 U.S. 39 (1968), overruling United States v. Kahriger, 345 U.S. 22 (1953) and Lewis v. United States, 348 U.S. 419 (1955).

132. Haynes v. United States, 390 U.S. 85 (1968).

133. Slochower v. Board of Higher Education of New York City, 350 U.S. 551 (1956).

134. Garrity v. New Jersey, 385 U.S. 493 (1967).

135. Spevack v. Klein, 385 U.S. 511 (1967), overruling Cohen v. Hurley, 366 U.S. 177 (1961).

136. Griffin v. California, 380 U.S. 609, 614 (1965), overruling Twining v. New Jersey, 211 U.S. 78 (1908) and Adamson v. California, 332 U.S. 46 (1947). The Court soon rejected the contention that comment is harmless error. Chapman v. California, 386 U.S. 18 (1967). In Tekan v. United States ex rel. Shott, 382 U.S. 406 (1966) the Court held that the rule of the Griffin case was not retroactive.

137. 384 U.S. 436.

138. McNabb v. United States, 318 U.S. 332 (1943).

139. Escobedo v. Illinois, 378 U.S. 478 (1964).

140. See David Fellman, *The Defendant's Rights Under English Law* (Madison: University of Wisconsin Press, 1966), pp. 34-45. See the comments of Justice Frankfurter in Culumbe v. Connecticut, 367 U.S. 568, 593-98 (1961).

141. See, e.g., People v. Dorado, 42 Cal. Rep. 169, 398 P. 2d 361 (1965).

142. 384 U.S. at 483.

143. Johnson v. New Jersey, 384 U.S. 719 (1966).

144. Evelle J. Younger, "Results of a Survey Conducted by the District Attorney's Office of Los Angeles County Regarding the Effect of the Miranda Decision upon the Prosecution of Felony Cases," *American Criminal Law Quarterly,* V (Fall, 1966), 32-39, see 33-34.

145. *Milwaukee Journal* (December 22, 1968).

146. Note, "Interrogations in New Haven: The Impact of Miranda," *Yale Law Journal,* LXXVI (July, 1967), 1519-1648.

147. Idem, pp. 1613-14.

148. Richard H. Seeburger and R. Stanton Wettick, Jr., "Miranda in Pittsburgh — A Statistical Study," *University of Pittsburgh Law Review,* XXIX (October, 1967), 1-26, see 26.

149. Richard J. Medalie, Leonard Zeitz, and Paul Alexander, "Custodial Police Interrogation in Our Nation's Capital: The Attempt to Implement Miranda," *Michigan Law Review,* LXVI (May, 1968), 1347-1422.

150. Cyril D. Robinson, "Police and Prosecutor Practices and Attitudes Relating to Interrogation as Revealed by Pre- and Post-Miranda Questionnaires: A Construct of Police Capacity to Comply," *Duke Law Journal,* MCMLXVIII (June, 1968), 425-524, see 495.

151. Idem, p. 506.

152. In re Gault, 387 U.S. 1 (1967). This decision was foreshadowed by Kent v. United States, 383 U.S. 541 (1966).

153. 387 U.S. at 18, 28.

154. Remmer v. United States, 347 U.S. 227 (1954); Pointer v. Texas, 380 U.S. 400 (1965); Douglas v. Alabama, 380 U.S. 415 (1965); Parker v. Gladden, 385 U.S. 363 (1966).

155. Bruton v. United States, 391 U.S. 123 (1968); Barber v. Page, 20 L. Ed. 2d 255 (1968).

156. Jencks v. United States, 353 U.S. 657 (1957).

157. In re Oliver, 333 U.S. 257 (1948).

158. Klopfer v. North Carolina, 386 U.S. 213 (1967). The Court has ruled that even if the accused is a prisoner in a federal penitentiary, a state which has a charge against him has a constitutional duty to make a diligent, good-faith effort to bring him before trial court without undue delay. Smith v. Hooey, 21 L. Ed. 2d 607 (1969).

159. Irvin v. Dowd, 366 U.S. 717 (1961); Sheppard v. Maxwell, 384 U.S. 333 (1966). Cf. Beck v. Washington, 369 U.S. 541 (1962).

160. Estes v. Texas, 381 U.S. 532 (1965); Rideau v. Louisiana, 373 U.S. 723 (1963).

161. Wright v. Georgia, 373 U.S. 284 (1963).

162. Pate v. Robinson, 383 U.S. 375 (1966).

163. Specht v. Patterson, 386 U.S. 605 (1967).

164. Washington v. Texas, 388 U.S. 14 (1967).

165. Griffin v. Illinois, 351 U.S. 12, 17 (1956).

166. 351 U.S. at 19.

167. 351 U.S. at 28.

168. Eskridge v. Washington State Board of Prison Terms and Paroles, 357 U.S. 214 (1958).

169. Draper v. State of Washington, 372 U.S. 487 (1963).

170. Lane v. Brown, 372 U.S. 477 (1963).

171. Hardy v. United States, 375 U.S. 277 (1964).

172. Bruns v. Ohio, 360 U.S. 252 (1959); Douglas v. Green, 363 U.S. 192 (1960).

173. Smith v. Bennett, 365 U.S. 708 (1961); Long v. District Court of Iowa, 385 U.S. 192 (1966).

174.   Coppedge v. United States, 369 U.S. 438 (1962).

175.   369 U.S. at 449. See Note, "Discriminations Against the Poor and the Fourteenth Amendment," *Harvard Law Review*, LXXXI (December, 1967), 435-53.

176.   See, e.g., Terry v. Ohio, 392 U.S. 1 (1968), upholding the validity of "stop-and-frisk" laws; Rogers v. United States, 340 U.S. 367 (1951), upholding a harsh waiver rule in respect to the privilege against self-incrimination; Bartkus v. Illinois, 359 U.S. 121 (1959), holding that the double jeopardy principle does not forbid putting a man on trial in a state court, on the charge of robbing a federally insured bank, after a previous trial and acquittal in a federal court based on the same event.

177.   See David R. Manwaring, "The Impact of Mapp v. Ohio," in David H. Everson, ed., *The Supreme Court as Policy-Maker: Three Studies on the Impact of Judicial Decisions* (Carbondale: Public Affairs Research Bureau, Southern Illinois University, 1968), pp. 1-43. Manwaring concluded that the Court has met "with only partial and very spotty success." Idem, p. 25.

178.   39 FRD 425.

179.   Escobedo v. Illinois, 378 U.S. 478, 499 (1964).

180.   Archibald Cox, *The Warren Court* (Cambridge: Harvard University Press, 1968), pp. 133-34.

7 Public Policy and the Control of Crime

Barbara N. McLennan

Kenneth McLennan

A successful strategy for fighting and reducing crime in the long run probably depends on some understanding of the causal factors associated with every different major class of crime. However, as Reiss has pointed out, our present crime reporting system is quite inadequate in terms of efficiency, accuracy, and national uniformity. At present, we have very little precise knowledge about social, economic, and psychological variables in every major criminal offense. Without this information, we cannot accurately assess the success of present crime prevention policies.

The problem of crime prevention is a matter of widespread national concern. Social research, which seeks to identify causative factors in various classes of crime, will depend on a substantial improvement in our techniques of crime reporting and analysis, and this task will be very difficult, costly, and time-consuming. Policy makers must seek solutions based on the data we have now, hoping, of course, that these data will be improved as time goes on. The information we now have therefore must serve as the basis for any general policy or strategy which aims toward the overriding goals of crime control and crime prevention.

The Geographic and Demographic Incidence of Crime

As indicated by Reiss, the incidence of crime can be a highly complex phenomenon. Some crimes can occur only if certain kinds of persons are present, and some types of locations are more definitely associated with certain kinds of crime than are others. Thus, burglaries can occur only where buildings are present, and rapes can occur only where females are present. This means, of course, that population distribution and urbanization are directly involved in all statistics on the nature and disposition of types of crime.

The Geographic Distribution of Crime

A great deal has been said about the increase in crime in large American cities, particularly the centers of those cities. Reiss notes several weaknesses in the usual manner of reporting the crime rate in these cities, but still concludes that the city is a very dangerous place and that, if anything, there is probably more crime than indicated in the usual statistics.

The President's Commission on Law Enforcement and Administration of Justice, in its widely read report, used the Uniform Crime Reports to

Table 4

Offenses Known by City Size, 1965 (per 100,000 population)

Group	Willful homicide	Forc- ible rape	Rob- bery	Aggra- vated assault	Bur- gla- ry	Larceny $50 and over	Motor vehicle theft
Cities over 1 million	10	26	221	246	930	734	586
500,000- 1 million	10	20	165	182	1,009	555	640
250,000- 500,000	7	15	122	142	1,045	550	468
100,000- 250,000	6	11	73	151	871	556	353
50,000- 100,000	4	8	49	85	675	492	297
25,000- 50,000	3	6	33	71	562	443	212
10,000- 25,000	2	6	19	67	462	309	141
Under 25,000	2	5	12	62	369	236	99
Rural	4	9	10	58	308	176	51
Suburban	3	10	26	66	545	359	160
All places	5	12	61	107	605	420	251

Source: President's Commission on Law Enforcement and Administration of Justice, *The Challenge of Crime in a Free Society* (Washington, D.C.: U.S.
Government Printing Office, 1967), p. 28.

compare criminal offenses by city size. (See Table 4). The President's Commission was struck by the number and extent of variations among the nation's cities, and noted that variations changed from crime to crime. It is true, however, that rural areas have generally lower crime rates than cities and that suburban rates, except for rape, are similar to those of small cities. Rates for most reported crimes (note Reiss's comments) are highest in the largest cities, although rates vary greatly from city to city. Thus, Los Angeles is the only city of over 1 million population which is among the 10 cities that have the highest rates for all index offenses. Newark, with the highest rate, is in the 250,000-500,000 category; Philadelphia ranked 51st, and New York ranked 28th.[1] An example is shown in the robbery rates (Table 5).

Table 5

Robbery Rates in 1965—14 Largest Cities in Order of Size
(per 100,000 population)

New York	114	Cleveland	213
Chicago	421	Washington	359
Los Angeles	293	St. Louis	327
Philadelphia	140	Milwaukee	28
Detroit	335	San Francisco	278
Baltimore	229	Boston	168
Houston	135	Dallas	79

Source: President's Commission on Law Enforcement and Administration of Justice, *The Challenge of Crime in a Free Society* (Washington, D.C.: U.S. Government Printing Office, 1967), p. 29.

Some of these variations are undoubtedly due to the fact that police practices and the quality of reporting vary from city to city. However, there are certain crimes, no matter how one criticizes and interprets current statistics, that are concentrated in big cities. These are, in particular, narcotic law violations, gambling, prostitution, and commercialized vice.[2] In addition, crime statistics show great variation among neighborhoods within large cities. Thus, rates of delinquency and adult crime are highest in the center of the city and decline as one moves away from the center. Also, crime rates are highest in the most deteriorated areas of the city—those areas characterized by "physical deterioration, declining population, high density, economic insecurity, poor housing, family disintegration, transiency, conflicting social norms, and an absence of constructive positive agencies."[3]

Demographic Dimensions of Crime

Because serious crimes occur most frequently in urban slum areas, the victimization rates in slum areas are much higher than in other areas. Also, because residents of urban slum areas tend to belong to certain minority groups, statistically the crime rate among these groups is much higher than the national average. Thus, the President's Commission tabulated statistics on victimization by race. (See Table 6.)

Table 6

Victimization by Race (per 100,000 population)

Offenses	White	Non-white
Total	1,860	2,592
Forcible rape	22	82
Robbery	58	204
Aggravated assault	186	347
Burglary	822	1306
Larceny ($50 and over)	608	367
Motor vehicle theft	164	286
Number of respondents	(27,484)	(4,902)

Source: President's Commission on Law Enforcement and Administration of Justice, *The Challenge of Crime in a Free Society* (Washington, D.C.: U.S. Government Printing Office, 1967), p. 39.

Non-whites in the United States are disproportionately victimized by all index crimes except larceny ($50 and over). Since non-whites in these residential areas comprise an economically deprived population, it can be said that the risk of victimization in the United States is highest for low-income groups, as summarized by the President's Crime Commission:

> . . . the risk of victimization is highest among the lower income groups for all index offenses except homicide, larceny, and vehicle theft; it weighs most heavily on the non-whites for all index offenses except larceny; it is borne by men more often than women, except, of course, for forcible rape, and the risk is greatest for the age category 20 to 29, except for larceny against women, and burglary, larceny, and vehicle theft against men.[4]

One implication of these data is that violent crimes are very frequently committed by individuals who are personally acquainted with their victims. In 1966 a survey of crime in the District of Columbia indicated that only 12 of 172 murders were interracial. Eighty-eight percent of rapes were committed by individuals against members of their own race. Only robbery, the single offense in which whites were victimized more than

Negroes, was predominantly interracial—in 56 percent of robberies committed by Negroes, the victims were white. (See Table 7.)

National arrest statistics are, in spite of the criticism Reiss and others have made of them, our basic source of information on who our criminals are. Based on these statistics, it is clear that most offenders in the United States are white, male, and over 24 years of age. Individuals over 24 comprise a very high proportion of all persons arrested for fraud, embezzlement, gambling, drunkenness, offenses against the family, and vagrancy. Other crimes are more frequently committed by younger age groups: burglaries, larcenies, and auto theft are most frequently committed by the 15-17 age group, and crimes of violence are most frequent in the 18-20 age group, with the 21-24 group close behind.[5]

Table 7

Victim-Offender Relationships, by Race and Sex, in Assaultive Crimes (except homicide)

| Victim Rate per 100,000 | Offenses Attributable to | | | | All offenders |
| | White | | Negro | | |
	Male	Female	Male	Female	
White males	201	9	129	4	342
White females	108	14	46	6	175
Negro males	58	3	1636	256	1953
Negro females	21	3	1202	157	1382
Total population	130	10	350	45	535

Source: President's Commission on Law Enforcement and Administration of Justice, *The Challenge of Crime in a Free Society* (Washington, D.C.: U.S. Government Printing Office, 1967), p. 40.

In comparing crime statistics by race, it is true that while more whites than Negroes are arrested, the Negro rate of arrest is much higher than the white in every offense category except certain public order and morals charges. As estimated by the President's Commission, "For index offenses plus larceny under $50, the rate per 100,000 Negroes in 1965 was four times as great as that for whites."[6] In addition, it is also true that the Negro rate for crimes of violence is higher than the white rate by a wider margin than for crimes of property. For example, the Negro murder rate is almost 10 times higher than the white rate, while the Negro burglary rate is only 3.5 times as high. While studies have shown that Negroes living under conditions similar to whites have similar (lower) crime rates, most Negroes live in poorer conditions, and comparisons are difficult to make. All of this is compounded by the fact that a very large percent of convicted criminals continue to commit crimes after being released from prison, so that once a person (Negro or white) is a criminal, he continues statistically to be counted the same way.[7]

Socioeconomic Environment of Criminal Behavior

The current level of crime and its geographic distribution significantly influence the quality of our urban life. Many persons believe that the extent of crime in urban communities is in some way related to other social problems which affect the urban environment. For example, there is clearly a relationship between some types of crime and high unemployment, poor housing, inadequate education, etc., but the precise causal factors are probably indeterminate. It is possible that no single socioeconomic variable is strongly correlated to the level of crime, but the complex configuration of many socioeconomic variables is likely to produce an environment which encourages crime. For example, the geographic distribution of unemployment does not coincide with the geographic distribution of crime. When the unemployment rate in major cities was less than 3 percent, the comparable rate for the Appalachian portion of West Virginia was 6.4 percent.[8] Undoubtedly, the crime rate in Appalachia for this period was much lower than in the urban centers. Similarly, a high crime rate cannot be attributed to the independent influence of poverty. In 1965 the chances of being poor were about one in four for rural residents, as compared with about one in six for residents of central cities.[9] It is therefore not feasible to claim that employment or poverty status explains the general level of crime. The explanation of high rates of urban crime is much more complex and involves not only absolute measure of income and employment status but also the extent of which urban residents experience discrimination in jobs, wages, and access to housing, education, and transportation within the urban community. Crime is also likely to be a function of the dynamic changes which occur within the central city as compared with the surrounding community. The nature and rate of mobility into and out of the central city influence the social environment, which determines the standards of behavior for the community.

Economic Factors

A community with a high unemployment rate will usually have a substantial proportion of its male work force without constructive activity to perform during the day. The result of unemployment usually is highly visible within the community. High unemployment communities in urban areas are likely to have substantial numbers-racket activity (a pursuit of those trying to make a living without a job) and a high rate of crime motivated by economic necessity (petty theft and purse snatching, etc.).

Teenage unemployment may also have an important influence on the rate of some forms of crime. In an urban ghetto with a one-third of a million population, a teenage unemployment rate of 30-40 percent may represent a pool of some 8,000-11,000 youths 16-19 years of age living in perhaps a 10-square-block area with virtually nothing to do all day and night. It is therefore not surprising that the rate of crimes of violence from gang activities, assault, commercial property theft, and car theft is high in central cities with one or more large ghettos.

Similar arguments can be used to explain the expected relationship between the level of income and some forms of crime. If the incidence of poverty is particularly high within local urban communities, these communities are likely to experience higher-than-average rates of crime involving petty theft, property damage, etc.

Economic statistics on unemployment are not available for the same geographic crime reporting areas. Consequently, it is not possible to correlate economic factors with the crime rates for local communities. The available data do, however, suggest that the central cities are in fact the high crime rate areas and that proportionately more crime is committed by non-whites.

Table 8 shows that since 1960, the unemployment rate for the population living in urban areas has fallen. This improvement has been experien-

Table 8

Unemployment Rates for Metropolitan Areas, by Race and Age

	1960 Metropolitan areas	1968 Metropolitan areas	Ghetto areas[a]
16 years and over	5.2	3.7	——
White	4.6	3.2	——
Negro	10.0	7.2	16.2
16-19 years	——	——	——
White	10.4	11.1	——
Negro	21.1	28.5	42.9

[a]Watts, Los Angeles, is taken as representative of ghetto unemployment.

Source: Data from U.S. Department of Labor survey of employment and unemployment as presented by Conrad Taeuber, U.S. Bureau of the Census, in testimony before the House Committee on Banking and Currency, October 14, 1969; Watts data are from U.S. Department of Labor, Bureau of Labor Statistics, *Urban Employment Survey,* 1969.

ced by both blacks and whites. However, the rate for black Americans, who tend to be located in the central core of the metropolitan area, is significantly higher than for white residents, who tend to be more widely distributed throughout the urban area. Unemployment rates of 7-10 percent among residents concentrated in the relatively small, densely populated geographic area of the central city make the unemployment problem highly visible and magnify its social impact on the community. The comparison with the apparently widespread affluence of the suburban ring is likely to generate among central city residents a feeling of distrust of the social system, including its economic and political institutions.

Within the central core of most large cities one or more sectors of extremely high unemployment are frequently found. These ghetto areas vary in size, from perhaps some 20,000 to half a million residents in the ghettos of very large cities. As indicated in Table 8, the unemployment rate in one ghetto in 1969 was 16.2 percent. Even among those working a substantial proportion, perhaps a third, are underemployed, in the sense that they are working less than a full day or a full week.

The problem of youth unemployment is even more serious than for the other labor force groups. While the overall unemployment rate has been falling since 1960, the rate for youths has in fact risen, and in ghetto areas has reached the incredible rate of over 40 percent. It is not surprising that the rate is high, since many youths enter, leave, and reenter the labor force. Similarly, job mobility is high among young workers as they experiment with various types of jobs. However, it is of some concern that the youth unemployment rate is rising while the overall rate is falling. It is not known whether this substantial pool of unemployed youths is made up of the same individuals for considerable periods of time. If the composition of the unemployment pool does not change rapidly, then the central city will be inhabited by a semipermanent corps of youths who are likely to see little justice in the present allocation of wealth, job opportunities, etc., and are likely to challenge every social and political institution in the central city.

Residents of the suburbs have a higher median family income than central city residents. This is particularly pronounced in the case of white residents. The median family income for Negroes has risen significantly since 1960 and is slightly higher for suburban Negroes than for Negroes in the central city. There is, of course, a substantial difference between Negro and white family income, and this is likely to encourage Negroes to question the social system which permits this inequality to exist.

Table 9 shows that the incidence of poverty is high for Negroes in both the central city and the suburbs. Almost one-third of the Negro central city residents are poor, and this reinforces their opposition to political authority within the city.

Substandard housing is found throughout the SMSA (standard metropolitan area) and is not confined to the central city. In fact, the available data suggest that housing conditions are somewhat worse outside the central city, at least for Negroes. The most interesting finding is that a significantly higher proportion of Negro housing units are substandard when compared with white housing units. It is, of course, not clear what relationship, if any, this finding has to the extent of urban crime. All that can be inferred is that the physical living conditions for at least 10-16 percent of urban Negro families are extremely poor, and that this will affect the social environment in which millions of young blacks grow up.

Table 9

Median Family Income, Incidence of Poverty, and Poor Housing, by Location and Race, 1960 and 1968

	Central City 1960	Central City 1968	Percent change	Suburban Ring 1960	Suburban Ring 1968	Percent change
Median income:						
White population	7160	8294	16	7791	9497	22
Negro population	4390	5623	28	3985	5857	47
Proportion population below poverty level:b						
White population	15	10	-33	11	6	-44
Negro population	43	30	-23	52	28	-46
Proportion of housing substandard:b						
All housing units	10	5	-50	9	4	-55
Negro units	25	10	-60	43	16	-63

aPoverty definition (as developed by the Social Security Administration) is based on the minimum food and other needs of the family, taking into account family size and farm-nonfarm residence. The poverty threshold for a nonfarm family of four was $3,335 in 1967 and $3,060 in 1959.

bThe data outside the central city are somewhat broader than the suburban ring. All units in SMSA, excluding the central city, are covered in the survey. This estimate underestimated the extent of substandard housing, since many more units do not meet local housing code standards.

Source: Conrad Taeuber, U.S. Bureau of the Census, in testimony before the House Committee on Banking and Currency, October 14, 1969.

Social Factors

There are at least two social factors which are likely to be indirect influences on the extent of crime in urban areas. These factors are the cohesiveness and stability of the local community and the extent to which parents are able to provide children with a standard of morality which coincides with the mores of the larger society.

If there is a high turnover in the population of a community, it is harder to build community interest groups which will influence the standards of behavior of those in the community. The problem of high turnover is magnified when the socioeconomic and racial characteristics of those leaving the community are different from the characteristics of those entering. This leads to the obvious problems of conflict within the community over economic property interests, racial integration, quality of public services, including education, and the financing of these services. In addition, the interest-group structure, which previously responded to community needs and in turn performed a leadership role in the community, may be unable to perform this function when the composition of the community is changing rapidly. Consequently, it may be difficult to mobilize community support for reducing such crimes as gang warfare, auto thefts, drug trafficking, etc. Experience has shown that central city communities are demanding better police services, but there is some question as to the extent to which the community itself is being mobilized to participate with the law enforcement officers in reducing crime.

As shown in Table 10, between 1960 and 1968 the central cities gained nearly two-thirds of a million people. As part of this net change the Negro population has increased by over 2 million, while the white population has declined by a little less than 2 million. About one-third of the increase in Negro central city population (800,000 persons) is due to net in-migration, while almost all of the white decline is due to net out-migration.

Most of the growth in the total Negro population since 1960 has occurred in the central cities. Most Negroes (about 55 percent) now reside in central cities, while only about 25 percent of whites live in central cities. These population shifts have certainly had a role in creating some current urban social problems. The social disintegration of neighborhoods, and the adjustment problems of the in-migrants in an environment already afflicted by high unemployment and poor housing are likely to result in an increase in the crime level in central cities.

It is widely believed that the household environment is extremely influential in determining a child's personality, motivation, and perception of

institutions in the community. It also is frequently asserted t
generally easier for the child to be imbued with positive motivation,
perceptions, etc., if the father is present in the household. The economic
problem faced by the female head of the household is severe and frequently results in little time being spent with children, and in many cases
even though some influence is exercised, it may in fact be detrimental to
the child's social and educational development.

If the role of the male is as important as is frequently alleged, then
the trend in the number of households headed by women is disquieting.
In the central cities in 1960, 10 percent of the white households were
headed by women, while some 23 percent of the Negro households were
headed by women. By 1963, there was a slight increase in the same figure
for white households. However, of Negro households in the central city,
nearly one-third are headed by women.[10] This is a very serious development, since the probability of these families being able to avoid poverty
is quite small. It must therefore be concluded that the trend in the central
city social environment is likely to continue to contribute to the rising
urban crime rate.

Table 10

Population of the United States, by Residence and Race, 1960 and 1968
(in millions)

Residence and race	1960	1968	Percent change
Total	178.5	198.2	11.1
Metropolitan areas	112.9	127.5	12.9
Central cities	57.8	58.4	1.0
Outside central cities	55.1	69.1	25.4
Nonmetropolitan	65.6	70.8	7.9
White:			
Metropolitan	99.7	110.9	11.2
Central cities	47.5	45.6	-3.9
Outside central cities	52.3	65.3	24.9
Negro:			
Metropolitan	12.2	15.1	24.3
Central cities	9.7	11.9	22.9
Outside central cities	2.5	3.2	29.8

Source: Conrad Taeuber, U.S. Bureau of the Census, in testimony before the
House Committee on Banking and Currency, October 14, 1969, Appen-
dixes.

Crime and the Urban Ghetto

The relationship of the socioeconomic environment to crime rates can be demonstrated when one analyzes the character and prevalence of crime in one actual urban ghetto. The Spring Garden area of Philadelphia is one such region. Here, almost all housing was constructed before 1939 and almost all residents live in extreme poverty. Between 80 percent and 90 percent of the population of the area (some 15,500 persons) are either Negro or Puerto Rican. In 1960, the annual family income for the Spring Garden area was about $2,700—well below the national (and Philadelphia) average.[11]

Spring Garden is an old and historic area of Philadelphia which once housed the wealthy, but it has been a slum since before 1950. Housing is inadequate in terms of both quantity and general condition, and the area is now very densely populated. It has few industrial establishments, no transportation facilities, and very inadequate recreational facilities.

In terms of socioeconomic standards, Spring Garden is quite different, statistically, from the rest of urban Philadelphia. In Spring Garden 11 percent of the adults have been divorced or separated, compared with 6 percent for the entire city; the median number of school years is 8.4, compared with 9.6 for the city. In 1960 the unemployment rate in the ghetto was twice as high as the city average; male unemployment in Spring Garden was 15.8 percent. Income was very low in Spring Garden compared with the rest of the city—47 percent of the families in the ghetto had incomes of under $3,000, compared with 17 percent for the whole city. Twenty-two percent of the residents of Spring Garden live on public welfare, compared with 5 percent for all of Philadelphia.[12]

Crime in Spring Garden is also greater than the citywide average. Rates for all crimes, except manslaughter, larceny under $50, and embezzlement, are higher than for the rest of the city.

It can be seen from Table 11 that residents of the ghetto are more prone to commit many types of crime than is the average city resident. It also is true that some crimes are more indicative of this generalization than others are.

For example, crimes related to physical violence (murder, aggravated assault, weapons) occur at a much higher rate in the ghetto than in the city. The difference in rate in these crimes is much greater than the difference in crimes related to property (robbery, larceny). Also, crimes related to social difficulties, family disintegration, and broad psychological problems are much more prevalent in the ghetto (prostitution, narcotics, drunkenness, offenses against the family).

Table 11

Crime Rates in Spring Garden
Compared with Philadelphia as a Whole, 1967
(per 100,000 population)

Type of crime	Philadelphia	Spring Garden	Percent difference
Crimes of violence:			
Murder	11	24	118.2
Manslaughter	7	3	-57.1
Rape	22	30	36.4
Aggravated assault	163	239	46.6
Assault	301	351	16.6
Weapons	90	233	158.9
Property crimes:			
Robbery	141	169	19.8
Burglary	603	848	46.0
Larceny, $50 and over	194	230	18.6
Larceny, under $50	788	248	-5.1
Auto theft	332	387	16.6
Arson	12	30	150.0
Forgery and counterfeiting	11	12	9.1
Fraud	27	33	22.2
Embezzlement	1.5		
Stolen property	5	9	80.0
Vandalism	281	290	4.2
Crimes reflecting personal psychological problems:			
Prostitution	23	78	239.1
Sex offenses	99	103	4.0
Narcotic drug laws	75	209	178.7
Gambling	273	354	29.7
Offenses again the family	17	36	111.8
Driving while intoxicated	95	103	8.4
Liquor laws	247	354	43.3
Drunkenness	1901	3496	83.9
Disorderly conduct	147	184	25.2
Vagrancy	23	24	4.3
Other:			
Suspicion	3201	3812	19.1
Traffic violations	114	160	40.3
All others	912	1510	65.6

Source: "Report on the Spring Garden Area," Part I (Philadelphia: Smith, Kline and French, August, 1968), p. 34. Report prepared under the supervision of W. L. Grala and G. Gumpert of Smith, Kline and French Corp. (Mimeographed.)

While the above statistics do not show any causal relationship, they do indicate that a relationship does exist between socioeconomic environment and specific types of crime. Those crimes which seem directly related to psychological problems are more prevalent among people living in a slum environment than among others. Physical decay, coupled with poverty and family disintegration, seems to infect people with a tendency toward violence or toward other psychological outlets for their deep-seated difficulties (e.g., alcohol, narcotics). This seems to be more clearly the case than any relationship between poverty or unemployment and crimes against property; while these rates are also high, they do not appear to be as different from the urban average as do the other criminal offenses. In any case, poverty and ghetto residence go together, and both are obviously involved in the higher ghetto crime rates.

Economic Rationale for Crime Control Strategy

The recent increased budget appropriation to fight the war on crime raises important questions about the appropriate strategy to follow. Although the distribution of this budget among the various forms of crime is partially a political decision, it should be supported by some form of economic rationale; otherwise, crime prevention resources will be wasted.

The Mix of Crime Prevention Services

Rottenberg points out that from society's point of view the eradication of all crime can be too expensive to undertake. Following a similar method, Rottenberg's analysis can be used to form the strategy for determining the mix of crime prevention services which society should supply. The rate at which crime prevention costs vary with the crime rate will be different for each class of crime. For example, Figure 1 shows two crimes, A and B. If the present crime rate is assumed to be the maximum of 100 percent, the expenditure of funds in the prevention of either crime will result in a lower rate for each crime. At some level of the reduced crime rate, the cost of further reduction will increase very rapidly and, as Rottenberg suggests, become prohibitive. However, as suggested in the figure, some crimes can be reduced substantially (crime A) before costs rise rapidly; for some other crimes (e.g., crime B), rising costs are experienced very early in the war on crime.

The illegal use of marijuana may fall into the crime B category. The deployment of crime prevention resources at points of entry into the country can probably reduce the supply of marijuana and raise its resale price in the nation's cities. This will reduce the quantity of "pot" demand-

Figure 1
Hypothetical Crime Prevention Costs

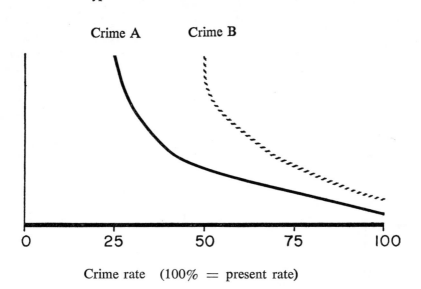

Crime rate   (100% = present rate)

ed. However, since the illegal act of consumption (as opposed to trafficking) is usually committed in private and does little damage to third parties, it is extremely difficult to detect. Further reduction of this crime rate, therefore, would require the assignment of a substantially more narcotics investigation personnel to major cities, with little likelihood of results. The appropriate strategy is therefore likely to involve stopping the expenditure of resources on crime B before they are stopped on crime A.

A knowledge of the cost level of crime relationship is not in itself enough to provide an economic rationale for crime prevention strategy. As Rottenberg has pointed out, it is also important to have an estimate of the benefits of crime prevention for each type of crime. Such benefits include the avoidance of costs caused by criminal acts; i.e., the cost of property destroyed by criminals or in their capture, loss of victims' earnings, and the costs of operating the criminal justice system.

The economic rationale in the cost-benefit ratio is frequently expressed by recommending that resources be allocated to crime prevention so long as benefits exceed costs and up to the point where extra (marginal) benefits equal extra (marginal) costs. Figure 2 illustrates this optimizing strategy. The figure assumes that there are three crimes and, for simplicity, that the marginal cost is constant. For the first crime the marginal benefits decline quickly and fall below the marginal cost of X. The optimum dollar cost allocated to preventing this crime is OA. Similarly, OB and OC represent the crime prevention funds which should be allocated to the other two crimes.

Figure 2

Hypothetical Cost-Benefit
Relationship for Several Crimes

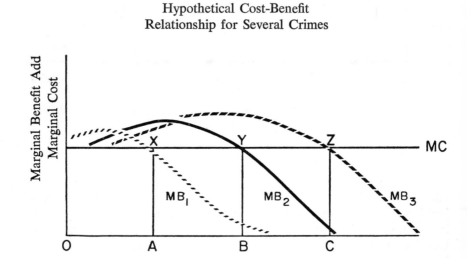

There is, of course an important difficulty with this approach to the crime-prevention mix problem. It assumes that the total crime prevention budget is flexible up to the equilibrium position of marginal cost-marginal benefit equality. As a practical matter, the size of this budget is determined in the political process, and its size may not allow the equilibrium position for each class of crime to be achieved. (The optimum size of the total crime prevention budget of course depends on the comparative cost-benefit relationship for all public services. More funds allocated to crime prevention may mean less for education, health, etc.

There may, therefore, be a sound economic explanation for the crime prevention budget being insufficient to optimize the expenditure on each class of crime.) For each crime it is therefore necessary to estimate the costs of benefits of the various levels of prevention effort. This approach, which attempts to simulate the benefits of different levels of effort, provides the optimum mix of crime prevention, given the limited total budget available.

Supply of Crime Prevention Services

Crime prevention services designed to reduce a specific crime frequently have substantial spill-over effects on other crimes. For example, if a city decides to crack down on the numbers racket by assigning more police on the beat in a densely populated neighborhood, the result will not be just reduced numbers racket activities—but the robbery rate is also likely to fall. This additional benefit must therefore be estimated when evaluating a strategy which focuses on reducing a specific crime. Similarly, technical improvements in a statewide communications system linking all police departments may be installed because of a high rate of armed robbery, but such a system will assist in the detection of many types of crimes.

A related feature of crime prevention expenditures is that the criminal will reallocate his efforts among different criminal activities. Consequently, optimizing with respect to each class of crime separately will not in general give an overall optimum with equal marginal benefits from prevention expenditures on each class of crime. (This point was suggested by J. R. Norsworthy, Department of Economics, Temple University.) It is for this reason that a simulation of the costs and benefits for all classes of crime is required.

The means used to supply crime prevention services may emphasize sophisticated equipment which embodies new crime detection methods (capital-intensive), or heavy reliance may be placed on the number of policemen per unit of population (labor-intensive). For some crimes the labor-intensive approach will be more effective, while for others the capital-intensive method is more likely to be used. If local communities decide to raise police salaries and improve the quality of the police force by raising entry standards, the higher labor costs will eventually result in communities substituting capital-intensive crime prevention techniques for work done by policemen. Any policy which advocates raising the quality of our police must follow the logical impact of this policy on the prevention of various types of crimes. In some instances it will induce the use and operation of sophisticated technical processes; for others (such as petty theft, mugging, etc.) it will simply raise the cost of crime prevention with little increase (if any) in the arrests per unit of population.

Joint Supply of Crime

In all industries there are economies of scale and advantages of horizontal and vertical integration. The crime industry is no exception. The same criminals may run the numbers and operate the prostitution service. The shake-down racket may be connected to either or both of these types of crime.

These characteristics of the crime industry have important implications for the war on crime. The tendency for the scale of operations to increase for some types of crime means that the apprehension of a criminal is likely to mean the exit of a considerable crime producer. On the other hand, the large criminal organization is likely to be in a strong position to influence the criminal justice system and reduce the consequences of apprehension.

The joint nature of the supply of some types of crime makes it difficult to legalize one type of crime while enforcing the law against another type of crime. For example, Rottenberg questions the advisability of making prostitution a crime. However, if prostitution and the shake-down racket are joint products, making the former legal may encourage increased shake-down activities.

Policy Recommendations

It is now widely acknowledged that crime, particularly violent crime, has reached such extensive proportions in urban American society that something substantial must be done about it quickly, or the life of our major population centers will be significantly and permanently impaired. Different points of view with respect to the issue, however, have led to widely divergent approaches to policy in this area.

The most commonly proposed solutions refer to traditional areas of our judicial and law enforcement systems. Individual laws can now be amended on the local and national levels to provide a somewhat more efficient apprehension and adjudication process. More police can be put on the streets, not only to arrest criminals but also to deter crime by would-be offenders. Greater resources can also be placed in police hands to improve police service programs. Research can be expanded in correctional programs, in an attempt to improve the rate of success of our present system of rehabilitation and to reduce the number of habitual offenders.

More can be done to alert our population to methods of preventing crime. Finally, it is now possible, through technical changes in current law, to improve the speed and efficiency of our present criminal court system.[13] All of these proposals, however, tend to have noncontroversial goals and would, by themselves, probably not have widespread immediate impact on current problems.

Vocal attacks upon decisions of the Warren Court have, for many, focused attention on the general antiquity and inefficiency of our current law enforcement process. As pointed out by Fellman, the United States Supreme Court has not really transformed American criminal law. It has merely, in a variety of matters, extended the intent of the federal Bill of Rights to apply to state law. An accused criminal in the courts of the United States is still very much the disadvantaged contestant: he must defend himself against the legal and physical resources of the established government—the police, the FBI, the district attorney's office et al.

While some change has, in very recent years, been made in the interpretation of American criminal law by the courts, very few changes have concurrently been made in our correctional system, in court procedures, in police organization and technology.[14] In Pennsylvania the current Crimes Code was enacted in 1860, when the state was 89 percent rural. It is now 80 percent urban. The 450 crimes in the Crimes Code could now be reclassified into 150 separate offenses, and many archaic laws could be omitted (as estimated by the Pennsylvania Crime Commission). Similarily, in Pennsylvania the Philadelphia State Correctional Institution was opened in 1829, and most other prisons in the state were also built in the early and mid-19th century. Police methods also are technologically out of date. It is now estimated, for example, that the Pennsylvania State Police teletype system, which is over 40 years old, can contact only 125 of 1,150 police departments in the state. Also, the regular equipment of the individual policemen (revolver, handcuffs, and baton) has not changed since the turn of the century.[15] Many other states have a similar record.

As Clark has amply demonstrated, the problem of gun control in the United States is today far different and far more extensive than when police organizations were first issued their regulation revolvers. A policeman today, with his 60-year-old personal arsenal, may be at a distinct disadvantage in dealing with both adult and juvenile offenders. If any great impact is to be made in the area of violent crime—homicide, assault, robbery—control of arms and ammunition will have to be a high-priority policy at all levels of administration in this country. This is essential in improving the effectiveness of current police forces.

Of course, it is also essential that other types of modern technology equal to that available to the professional criminal be placed in the hands of our law enforcement agencies. Sills has discussed some of the elements of controversy involved in the problems of using wiretapping at the federal and state levels. Innovation in communications and data collection is additionally, and less controversially, required at a more basic level in the enforcement process. The introduction and use of computers to compile data is essential if the enforcement agencies are to keep pace with the criminals. The development of a truly accurate and uniform crime reporting system is also necessary in the long run, if any national exchange of information is effectively to take place. All this takes a great deal of research, and a great deal of money.

The problem facing policymakers is to determine the most efficient strategy by which to attack the crime problem. Policymakers have only a limited amount of resources at their disposal in this decision, and must evaluate their choice in terms of the costs and savings involved. Gun control would be a policy of relatively small economic cost from the general taxpayer's viewpoint. Enacting gun control legislation is a political issue, involving political debts and special interests, and has relatively little to do with economic costs to the general community. In other words, in economic terms gun control would probably save the community more in crime reduction and prevention than it would cost the manufacturers and salesmen of firearms. The choice thus far in this area has been politically rather than economically motivated.

In contrast, some proposed crime prevention policies could be very costly. Increasing the size of local police forces and improving their quality is one such policy, because this is a labor-intensive industry. This policy would entail higher salaries and greater benefits to large numbers of policemen, longer and better-managed training programs, and the distribution of expensive technological equipment. Similarly, the widespread use of psychological and psychiatric methods, i.e., treating all crime as a form of disease, would be exorbitant in cost. It would necessitate the training and utilization of a massive labor force of psychologists, psychiatrists, diagnosticians, etc.

In addition, as suggested by Rottenberg, it is possible that legal codes may be revised so that archiac laws can be dropped. In conjunction with this, it is worth considering the suggestion that acts in which no third party is hurt (e.g., gambling, some other traditional vices) not be considered crimes at all.

In the long run, undoubtedly, only broad social policies can have great impact on the extent of crime in this country. This would involve a complete program of education, manpower training, and some method of guaranteeing the level of income. Only a strategy such as this can get at the basic sources of crime—economic insecurity, antisocial behavior, and the predisposition to use violence for selfish personal benefit.

Some Specific Recommendations

We know, from what these and other authors have told us, that crime in the United States is widespread, concentrated in our urban centers, committed in a disproportional number of cases by members of minority groups, and difficult to control. Traditional policy approaches which stress improvement of the police and broad social policies, while of very high priority and of long-term necessity, will be very costly, and their results will be slow in being assessed. In addition to these approaches, it is also possible to make some impact on the crime statistics by legislating changes in certain current practices.

One such policy would be to legalize such minor vices as the numbers racket. There apparently exists a widespread demand in certain communities for an opportunity to gamble very small amounts on frequent occasions and to be paid off with equal regularity and frequency (maximum of about one week between the wager and the payoff), though in relatively small amounts. The experimentation some states have conducted with respect to state lotteries does not really tap this market. State lotteries tend to make individual bets quite expensive, and payoffs may in some places take as long as six months.

A numbers racket is in one sense a local small business. It is true that criminal elements currently manage this racket, as they do other vices. There may be a connection between the incidence of numbers and such activities as prostitution. Legalization of numbers may mean a spread in prostitution. However, it is more efficient for local police forces to try to deal with one crime than with two, and control of prostitution is less costly than control of numbers.

Like a state lottery, a numbers racket (unlike other vices) can be turned to local community advantage. Eliminating the criminal element from its management will eliminate the risk of harm to innocent third parties and make these transactions into businesslike arrangements between consumers and those selling the service. If local communities ran the industry themselves (as, for example, some states sell hard liquor in state stores in the local communities), a substantial amount of revenue would be raised by local government which is today the property of organized crime.

A second specific recommendation lies in the area of corrections. Obviously it is more efficient and less costly to prevent crime than to deal with its results. A rational corrections system would differentiate the youthful offender from the older, hardened criminal. We know that a high percentage of crime is committed by recidivists, persons who as soon as they are released from prison commit the same sort of crime for which they have already been convicted. It is much more efficient for society to keep these individuals in prison while focusing rehabilitation programs on those who are young enough, if trained, to live useful lives and contribute something to society. An older man, if retrained, even if he could be rehabilitated (certainly not the most hopeful area for correctional activity), would not have much time to make such a contribution.

Another area of crime which could be directly affected by specific current changes lies in the area of teenage and juvenile crime. We know that a large percentage of youthful crime consists of auto thefts. The number of thefts could be significantly reduced if states would require all new autos to have self-locking steering mechanisms as an anti-crime device. Also, to handle older cars, states could make it a traffic violation to leave automobiles unlocked. This latter policy would be more costly, since it would involve hiring more individuals, such as meter maids, to police the new regulation.

These are only a small number of possible recommendations; obviously many others of similar range can be made and applied in various state criminal systems. Such recommendations, to have any validity, however, must be based on a general strategy or approach to crime prevention. They must demonstrate an awareness of the relevant social, economic, and psychological factors. Simply to provide for greater public expenditures at all levels of government (e.g., for more police or more socioeconomic programs of the same type we have had), without a new rationale, would be to overlook the basic failures of past approaches. A successful strategy must be based on a close-reasoned analysis of the problem and must utilize all the information we have that relates to the problem of crime.

Notes

1. President's Commission on Law Enforcement and Administration of Justice, *The Challenge of Crime in a Free Society* (Washington, D.C.: U.S. Government Printing Office, 1967), p. 29.

2. Marvin E. Wolfgang, "Urban Crime," in *The Metropolitan Enigma* (Washington, D.C.: Chamber of Commerce of the U.S., 1967), p. 241.

3. Ibid., quoting Clifford R. Shaw and Henry D. McKay, *Juvenile Delinquency and Urban Areas* (Chicago: University of Chicago Press, 1942). Also noted by the President's Commission, op. cit., pp. 35-37.

4. President's Commission, op. cit., p. 39.

5. Ibid., p. 44.

6. Ibid.

7. Ibid.

8. Based on report of the Appalachian Regional Commission, as quoted in Niles Hanson, "Geographic Dimensions of Manpower Policy" (1969). (Mimeographed.)

9. Based on data contained in President's National Advisory Commission on Rural Poverty, *The People Left Behind* (Washington, D.C.: U.S. Government Printing Office, 1967), p. 3.

10. Conrad Taeuber, U.S. Bureau of the Census, in testimony before the House Committee on Banking and Currency, October 14, 1969; Watts data are from U.S. Department of Labor, Bureau of Labor Statistics, *Urban Employment Survey, 1969.* Appendix.

11. "Report on the Spring Garden Area," Part I (Philadelphia: Smith, Kline and French, August, 1968). Report prepared under the supervision of W. L. Grala and G. Gumpert of Smith, Kline and French Corp. (Mimeographed.)

12. Ibid., pp. 17-31.

13. These policies were advanced by James A. Wilson, in "Crime and Law Enforcement," in Kermit Gorden, ed., *Agenda for the Nation* (Washington, D.C.: Brookings Institution, 1968), pp. 205-06.

14. Point made by J. Shane Creamer, Director, Pennsylvania Crime Commission, at a conference held at Temple University, April 1, 1969.

15. *Goals for Justice,* Task Force Report of the Pennsylvania Crime Commission (Harrisburg, 1969), pp. 17-18.

About the Editor

Barbara N. McLennan is Associate Professor of Political Science at Temple University, and a member of the International Studies Association, the American Political Science Association and the Association for Asian Studies. She has published articles in "World Review," "International Review of History and Political Science," "Journal of Asian and African Studies," "Journal of Southeast Asian History," "Africa Quarterly," "Journal of Southeast Asian History," and "Il Politico." Professor McLennan is a graduate of the City College of the City of New York and holds a Ph.D. degree from the University of Wisconsin.

About the Contributors

Joseph S. Clark, former United States Senator from Pennsylvania, is President of the World Federalists, U.S.A., and Chairman of the Coalition on National Priorities and Military Policy.

David Fellman is Vilas Professor of Political Science at the University of Wisconsin.

Kenneth McLennan is Associate Professor of Economics at Temple University.

W. Walter Menninger, M.D., is associated with the Menninger Foundation in Topeka, Kansas, and is a member of the National Commission on the Causes and Prevention of Violence.

Albert J. Reiss, Jr., is Professor of Sociology at the University of Michigan.

Simon Rottenberg is Professor of Economics at Duke University.

Arthur J. Sills, Attorney General of the state of New Jersey from January 1962 to January 1970 and former President of the National Association of Attorneys General, is a member of the law firm of Sills, Garretson, Levine, and Goceljack in Perth Amboy.